Modern Critical Interpretations

Emily Brontë's
Wuthering Heights

Modern Critical Interpretations

These and other titles in preparation

Emily Brontë's

Wuthering Heights

Edited and with an introduction by
Harold Bloom
Sterling Professor of the Humanities
Yale University

Chelsea House Publishers
NEW YORK ◇ PHILADELPHIA

31334000 351 458.

∞ The paper used in this publication meets the minimum
requirements of the American National Standard for
Permanence of Paper for Printed Library Materials,
Z39.48–1984.

Library of Congress Cataloging-in-Publication Data
Emily Brontë's Wuthering Heights.
    (Modern critical interpretations)
    Bibliography: p.
    Includes index.
    Summary: A collection of eight critical essays on Emily
Brontë's novel "Wuthering Heights" arranged in chronological
order of publication.
    1. Brontë, Emily, 1818–1848.   Wuthering Heights.
[1. Brontë, Emily, 1818–1848.   Wuthering Heights.
2. English literature—History and criticism]
I. Bloom, Harold.   II. Series
PR4172.W73E45   1986   823'.8   86-17149
ISBN 0-87754-737-7

823 BRONTE

Contents

Editor's Note

This book gathers together a representative selection of the best criticism available upon Emily Brontë's *Wuthering Heights,* arranged in the chronological order of its original publication. I am grateful to Jennifer Wagner and Susan Laity for their erudition and judgment in helping me to edit this volume.

The editor's introduction addresses itself to the Byronic influence upon the Brontë sisters, with particular emphasis upon *Wuthering Heights* as a triumphant revision of *Manfred,* a revision seen here as centering upon Emily Brontë's essentially Gnostic vision. Dorothy Van Ghent's daemonic reading begins the chronological sequence, and its influence can be felt in several of the later essays in this volume. For Van Ghent, the novel offers a duality of human or social existence, as well as a nonhuman realm of being, both reflected in the duality of the psyche in each of us. A very different argument is made by David Sonstroem, for whom the narrative is a study in the blindness of "several limited and inadequate points of view—genteel, Christian, pragmatic, animistic—at indecisive war with one another."

Frank Kermode, studying *Wuthering Heights* as a modern version of the classic, subtly reads it as an exercise in the economy of its characters' names, and finds in Heathcliff the romance's mediator: "neither inside nor out, neither wholly master nor wholly servant, the husband who is no husband, the brother who is no brother, the father who abuses his changeling child, the cousin without kin." If Kermode charts an economy of dearth and emptiness in the sparseness of the book's names, Margaret Homans traces a more Freudian economy of absence in her account of how nature undergoes both repression and sublimation in *Wuthering Heights.*

One of our leading feminist critics, Sandra M. Gilbert, analyzes the novel as Emily Brontë's quest for her own female origins in a kind of Blakean antithetical Fall, one that transposes and subverts normative values. Carol Jacobs, employing the resources of contemporary deconstruction, demonstrates how strange the relationship is between Lockwood's narrative and the tale the book is able to tell. This calls into question the apparent images of reconciliation that most critics find at the close of the novel.

In the final essay, Stevie Davies presents the suffering of the first Catherine, who dies in giving birth to the second, as a kind of myth of rebirth, Emily Brontë's dark wisdom being that "the happiness of the future . . . is built on the destruction of the past." The essay's last surmise, that Heathcliff mysteriously has given up some of his life to the second Catherine, is an insight much in Emily Brontë's own spirit, and fittingly concludes this volume.

Introduction

The three Brontë sisters—Charlotte, Emily Jane, and Anne—are unique literary artists whose works resemble one another's far more than they do the work of writers before or since. Charlotte's compelling novel *Jane Eyre* and her three lesser yet strong narratives—*The Professor, Shirley, Villette*—form the most extensive achievement of the sisters, but critics and common readers alike set even higher the one novel of Emily Jane's, *Wuthering Heights,* and a handful of her lyrical poems. Anne's two novels—*Agnes Grey* and *The Tenant of Wildfell Hall*—remain highly readable, although dwarfed by *Jane Eyre* and the authentically sublime *Wuthering Heights.*

Between them, the Brontës can be said to have invented a relatively new genre, a kind of northern romance, deeply influenced both by Byron's poetry and by his myth and personality, but going back also, more remotely yet as definitely, to the Gothic novel and to the Elizabethan drama. In a definite, if difficult to establish sense, the heirs of the Brontës include Thomas Hardy and D. H. Lawrence. There is a harsh vitalism in the Brontës that finds its match in the Lawrence of *The Rainbow* and *Women in Love,* though the comparison is rendered problematic by Lawrence's moral zeal, enchantingly absent from the Brontës' literary cosmos.

The aesthetic puzzle of the Brontës has less to do with the mature transformations of their vision of Byron into Rochester and Heathcliff, than with their earlier fantasy-life and its literature, and the relation of that life and literature to its hero and precursor, George Gordon, Lord Byron. At his rare worst and silliest, Byron has nothing like this scene from Charlotte Brontë's "Caroline Vernon," where Caroline confronts the Byronic Duke of Zamorna:

> The Duke spoke again in a single blunt and almost coarse sentence, compressing what remained to be said, "If I were a

1

bearded Turk, Caroline, I would take you to my harem." His deep voice as he uttered this, his high featured face, and dark, large eye burning bright with a spark from the depths of Gehenna, struck Caroline Vernon with a thrill of nameless dread. Here he was, the man Montmorency had described to her. All at once she knew him. Her guardian was gone, something terrible sat in his place.

Byron died his more-or-less heroic death at Missolonghi in Greece on April 19, 1824, aged thirty-six years and three months, after having set an impossible paradigm for authors that has become what the late Nelson Algren called "Hemingway all the way," in a mode still being exploited by Norman Mailer, Gore Vidal, and some of their younger peers. Charlotte was eight, Emily Jane six, and Anne four when the Noble Lord died and when his cult gorgeously flowered, dominating their girlhood and their young womanhood. Byron's passive-aggressive sexuality—at once sadomasochistic, homoerotic, incestuous, and ambivalently narcissistic—clearly sets the pattern for the ambiguously erotic universes of *Jane Eyre* and *Wuthering Heights*. What Schopenhauer named (and deplored) as the Will to Live, and Freud subsequently posited as the domain of the drives, is the cosmos of the Brontës, as it would come to be of Hardy and Lawrence. Byron rather than Schopenhauer is the source of the Brontës' vision of the Will to Live, but the Brontës add to Byron what his inverted Calvinism only partly accepted, the Protestant will proper, a heroic zest to assert one's own election, one's place in the hierarchy of souls.

Jane Eyre and Catherine Earnshaw do not fit into the grand array of heroines of the Protestant will that commences with Richardson's Clarissa Harlowe and goes through Austen's Emma Woodhouse and Fanny Price to triumph in George Eliot's Dorothea Brooke and Henry James's Isabel Archer. They are simply too wild and Byronic, too High Romantic, to keep such company. But we can see them with Hardy's Tess and, even more, his Eustacia Vye, and with Lawrence's Gudrun and Ursula. Their version of the Protestant will stems from the Romantic reading of Milton, but largely in its Byronic dramatization, rather than its more dialectical and subtle analyses in Blake and Shelley, and its more normative condemnation in Coleridge and in the Wordsworth of *The Borderers*.

II

Wuthering Heights is as unique and idiosyncratic a narrative as *Moby-Dick*, and like Melville's masterwork breaks all the confines of genre. Its sources, like the writings of the other Brontës, are in the fantasy literature of a very young woman, in the poems that made up Emily Brontë's Gondal saga or cycle. Many of those poems, while deeply felt, simply string together Byronic commonplaces. A few of them are extraordinarily strong and match *Wuthering Heights* in sublimity, as in the famous lyric dated January 2, 1846:

No coward soul is mine
No trembler in the world's storm-troubled sphere
I see Heaven's glories shine
And Faith shines equal arming me from Fear

O God within my breast
Almighty ever-present Deity
Life, that in me hast rest
As I Undying Life, have power in Thee

Vain are the thousand creeds
That move men's hearts, unutterably vain,
Worthless as withered weeds
Or idlest froth amid the boundless main

To waken doubt in one
Holding so fast by thy infinity
So surely anchored on
The steadfast rock of Immortality

With wide-embracing love
Thy spirit animates eternal years
Pervades and broods above,
Changes, sustains, dissolves, creates and rears

Though Earth and moon were gone
And suns and universes ceased to be
And thou wert left alone
Every Existence would exist in thee

There is not room for Death
Nor atom that his might could render void
Since thou art Being and Breath
And what thou art may never be destroyed.

We could hardly envision Catherine Earnshaw, let alone Heathcliff, chanting these stanzas. The voice is that of Emily Jane Brontë, addressing the God within her own breast, a God who certainly has nothing in common with the one worshipped by the Reverend Patrick Brontë. I do not hear in this poem, despite all its Protestant resonances, any nuance of Byron's inverted Miltonisms. *Wuthering Heights* seems to me a triumphant revision of Byron's *Manfred,* with the revisionary swerve taking Emily Brontë into what I would call an original gnosis, a kind of poetic faith, like Blake's or Emerson's, that resembles some aspects (but not others) of ancient Gnosticism without in any way actually deriving from Gnostic texts. "No coward soul is mine" also emerges from an original gnosis, from the poet's knowing that her *pneuma* or breath-soul, as compared to her less ontological psyche, is no part of the created world, since that world fell even as it was created. Indeed the creation, whether heights or valley, appears in *Wuthering Heights* as what the ancient Gnostics called the *kenoma,* a cosmological emptiness into which *we have been thrown,* a trope that Catherine Earnshaw originates for herself. A more overt Victorian Gnostic, Dante Gabriel Rossetti, made the best (if anti-feminist) observation on the setting of *Wuthering Heights,* a book whose "power and sound style" he greatly admired:

> It is a fiend of a book, an incredible monster, combining all the stronger female tendencies from Mrs. Browning to Mrs. Brownrigg. The action is laid in Hell,—only it seems places and people have English names there.

Mrs. Brownrigg was a notorious eighteenth-century sadistic and murderous midwife, and Rossetti rather nastily imputed to *Wuthering Heights* a considerable female sadism. The book's violence is astonishing but appropriate, and appealed darkly both to Rossetti and to his close friend, the even more sadomasochistic Swinburne. Certainly the psychodynamics of the relationship between Heathcliff and Catherine go well beyond the domain of the pleasure principle. Sandra M. Gilbert and Susan Gubar may stress too much that Heathcliff is Catherine's whip, the answer to her most profound fantasies, but the suggestion was Emily Brontë's before it became so fully developed by her best feminist critics.

Walter Pater remarked that the precise use of the term *romantic* did not apply to Sir Walter Scott, but rather:

> Much later, in a Yorkshire village, the spirit of romanticism bore a more really characteristic fruit in the work of a young girl, Emily Brontë, the romance of *Wuthering Heights;* the figures

of Hareton Earnshaw, of Catherine Linton, and of Heathcliff—tearing open Catherine's grave, removing one side of her coffin, that he may really lie beside her in death—figures so passionate, yet woven on a background of delicately beautiful, moorland scenery, being typical examples of that spirit.

I always have wondered why Pater found the Romantic spirit more in Hareton and the younger Catherine than in Catherine Earnshaw, but I think now that Pater's implicit judgment was characteristically shrewd. The elder Catherine is the problematical figure in the book; she alone belongs to both orders of representation, that of social reality and that of otherness, of the Romantic Sublime. After she and the Lintons, Edgar and Isabella, are dead, then we are wholly in Heathcliff's world for the last half-year of his life, and it is in that world that Hareton and the younger Catherine are portrayed for us. They are—as Heathcliff obscurely senses—the true heirs to whatever societally possible relationship Heathcliff and the first Catherine could have had.

Emily Brontë died less than half a year after her thirtieth birthday, having finished *Wuthering Heights* when she was twenty-eight. Even Charlotte, the family survivor, died before she turned thirty-nine, and the world of *Wuthering Heights* reflects the Brontë reality: the first Catherine dies at eighteen, Hindley at twenty-seven, Heathcliff's son Linton at seventeen, Isabella at thirty-one, Edgar at thirty-nine, and Heathcliff at thirty-seven or thirty-eight. It is a world where you marry early, because you will not live long. Hindley is twenty when he marries Frances, while Catherine Earnshaw is seventeen when she marries the twenty-one-year-old Edgar Linton. Heathcliff is nineteen when he makes his hellish marriage to poor Isabella, who is eighteen at the time. The only happy lovers, Hareton and the second Catherine, are twenty-four and eighteen, respectively, when they marry. Both patterns—early marriage and early death—are thoroughly High Romantic, and emerge from the legacy of Shelley, dead at twenty-nine, and of Byron, martyred to the cause of Greek independence at thirty-six.

The passions of Gondal are scarcely moderated in *Wuthering Heights,* nor could they be; Emily Brontë's religion is essentially erotic, and her vision of triumphant sexuality is so mingled with death that we can imagine no consummation for the love of Heathcliff and Catherine Earnshaw except death. I find it difficult therefore to accept Gilbert and Gubar's reading in which *Wuthering Heights* becomes a Romantic feminist critique of *Paradise Lost,* akin to Mary Shelley's *Frankenstein.* Emily Brontë is no more interested in refuting Milton than in sustaining him. What Gilbert and Gubar uncover in *Wuthering Heights* that is antithetical to *Paradise Lost* comes directly from Byron's *Manfred,* which certainly *is* a Romantic critique of *Paradise Lost.* *Wuthering Heights* is *Manfred* converted to prose romance, and Heathcliff is more like Manfred, Lara, and Byron himself than is Charlotte Brontë's Rochester.

Byronic incest—the crime of Manfred and Astarte—is no crime for Emily Brontë, since Heathcliff and Catherine Earnshaw are more truly brother and sister than are Hindley and Catherine. Whatever inverted morality—a curious blend of Catholicism and Calvinism—Byron enjoyed, Emily Brontë herself repudiates, so that *Wuthering Heights* becomes a critique of *Manfred,* though hardly from a conventional feminist perspective. The furious energy that is loosed in *Wuthering Heights* is precisely Gnostic; its aim is to get back to the original Abyss, before the creation-fall. Like Blake, Emily Brontë identifies her imagination with the Abyss, and her *pneuma* or breath-soul with the Alien God, who is antithetical to the God of the creeds. The heroic rhetoric of Catherine Earnshaw is beyond every ideology, every merely social formulation, beyond even the dream of justice or of a better life, because it is beyond this cosmos, "this shattered prison":

> "Oh, you see, Nelly! he would not relent a moment, to keep me out of the grave! *That* is how I'm loved! Well, never mind! That is not *my* Heathcliff. I shall love mine yet; and take him with me—he's in my soul. And," added she, musingly, "the thing that irks me most is this shattered prison, after all. I'm tired, tired of being enclosed here. I'm wearying to escape into that glorious world, and to be always there; not seeing it dimly through tears, and yearning for it through the walls of an aching heart; but really with it, and in it. Nelly, you think you are better and more fortunate than I; in full health and strength. You are sorry for me—very soon that will be altered. I shall be sorry for *you.* I shall be incomparably beyond and above you all. I *wonder* he won't be near me!" She went on to herself. "I thought he wished it. Heathcliff, dear! you should not be sullen now. Do come to me, Heathcliff."

Whatever we are to call the mutual passion of Catherine and Heathcliff, it has no societal aspect and neither seeks nor needs societal sanction. Romantic love has no fiercer representation in all of literature. But "love" seems an inadequate term for the connection between Catherine and Heathcliff. There are no elements of transference in that relation, nor can we call the attachment involved either narcissistic or anaclitic. If Freud is not applicable, then neither is Plato. These extraordinary vitalists, Catherine and Heathcliff, do not desire in one another that which each does not possess, do not lean themselves against one another, and do not even find and thus augment their own selves. They *are* one another, which is neither sane nor possible, and which does not support any doctrine of liberation whatsoever. Only that most extreme of visions, Gnosticism, could accommodate them, for like the Gnostic adepts Catherine and Heathcliff can only enter the *pleroma* or fullness together, as presumably they have done after Heathcliff's self-induced death by starvation.

Blake may have promised us the Bible of Hell; Emily Brontë seems to have disdained Heaven and Hell alike. Her finest poem (for which we have no manuscript, but it is inconceivable that it could have been written by Charlotte) rejects every feeling save her own inborn "first feelings" and every world except a vision of earth consonant with those inaugural emotions:

> Often rebuked, yet always back returning
> To those first feelings that were born with me,
> And leaving busy chase of wealth and learning
> For idle dreams of things which cannot be:
>
> To-day, I will seek not the shadowy region;
> Its unsustaining vastness waxes drear;
> And visions rising, legion after legion,
> Bring the unreal world too strangely near.
>
> I'll walk, but not in old heroic traces,
> And not in paths of high morality,
> And not among the half-distinguished faces,
> The clouded forms of long-past history.
>
> I'll walk where my own nature would be leading:
> It vexes me to choose another guide:
> Where the gray flocks in ferny glens are feeding;
> Where the wild wind blows on the mountain side.
>
> What have those lonely mountains worth revealing?
> More glory and more grief than I can tell:
> The earth that wakes *one* human heart to feeling
> Can centre both the worlds of Heaven and Hell.

Whatever that centering is, it is purely individual, and as beyond gender as it is beyond creed or "high morality." It is the voice of Catherine Earnshaw, celebrating her awakening from the dream of heaven:

> "I was only going to say that heaven did not seem to be my home; and I broke my heart with weeping to come back to earth; and the angels were so angry that they flung me out, into the middle of the heath on the top of Wuthering Heights; where I woke sobbing for joy."

On *Wuthering Heights*

Dorothy Van Ghent

Emily Brontë's single novel is, of all English novels, the most treacherous
for the analytical understanding to approach. It is treacherous not because
of failure in its own formal controls on its meaning—for the book is highly
wrought in form—but because it works as a level of experience that is
unsympathetic to, or rather, simply irrelevant to the social and moral reason.
One critic has spoken of the quality of feeling in this book as "a quality of
suffering":

> It has anonymity. It is not complete. Perhaps some ballads rep-
> resent it in English, but it seldom appears in the main stream,
> and few writers are in touch with it. It is a quality of experience
> the expression of which is at once an act of despair and an act
> of recognition or of worship. It is the recognition of an absolute
> hierarchy. This is also the feeling in Aeschylus. It is found
> amongst genuine peasants and is a great strength. Developing
> in places which yield only the permanent essentials of existence,
> it is undistracted and universal.

We feel the lack of "completeness," which this critic refers to, in the nature
of the dramatic figures that Emily Brontë uses: they are figures that arise
on and enact their drama on some ground of the psychic life where ethical
ideas are not at home, at least such ethical ideas as those that inform our
ordinary experience of the manners of men. They have the "anonymity"

From *The English Novel: Form and Function.* © 1953 by Dorothy Van Ghent. Holt,
Rinehart & Winston, 1953.

of figures in dreams or in religious ritual. The attitude toward life that they suggest is rather one of awed contemplation of an unregenerate universe than a feeling for values or disvalues in types of human intercourse. It is an attitude that is expressed in some of the great Chinese paintings of the Middle Ages, where the fall of a torrent from an enormous height, or a single huge wave breaking under the moon, or a barely indicated chain of distant mountains lost among mists, seems to be animated by some mysterious, universal, half-divine life which can only be "recognized," not understood.

The strangeness that sets *Wuthering Heights* apart from other English novels does not lie alone in the attitude that it expresses and the level of experience that it defines, for something of the same quality of feeling exists, for instance, in Conrad's work. Its strangeness is the perfect simplicity with which it presents its elemental figures almost naked of the web of civilized habits, ways of thinking, forms of intercourse, that provides the familiar background of other fiction. Even Conrad's adventurers, no matter how far they may go into the "heart of darkness," carry with them enough threads of this web to orient them socially and morally. We can illustrate what we mean by this simplicity, this almost nakedness, if we compare Emily Brontë's handling of her materials with Richardson's handling of materials that, in some respects, are similar in kind. For example, the daemonic character of Heathcliff, associated as it is with the wildness of heath and moors,, has a recognizable kinship with that of Lovelace, daemonic also, though associated with town life and sophisticated manners. Both are, essentialy, an anthropomorphized primitive energy, concentrated in activity, terrible in effect. But Emily Brontë insists on Heathcliff's gypsy lack of origins, his lack of orientation and determination in the social world, his equivocal status on the edge of the human. When Mr. Earnshaw first brings the child home, the child is an "it," not a "he," and "dark almost as if it came from the devil"; and one of Nelly Dean's last reflections is, "Is he a ghoul or a vampire?" But Richardson's Lovelace has all sorts of social relationships and determinations, an ample family economic orientation, college acquaintances, a position in a clique of young rakes; and Richardson is careful, through Lovelace's own pen, to offer various rationalizations of his behavior, each in some degree cogent. So with the whole multifold *Clarissa*-myth: on all sides it is supported for the understanding by historically familiar morality and manners. But *Wuthering Heights* is almost bare of such supports in social rationalization. Heathcliff might *really* be a demon. The passion of Catherine and Heathcliff is too simple and undeviating in its intensity, too uncomplex, for us to find in it any echo of practical social reality. To say that the motivation of this passion is "simple" is not to say that it is easy to define: much easier to define are the motivations that are somewhat complex and devious, for this is the familiar nature of human motivations. We might associate perfectly "simple" motivations with animal nature or extrahuman nature, but by the same token the quality of feeling involved would resist analysis.

But this nakedness from the web of familiar morality and manners is not quite complete. There is the framework formed by the convention of narration (the "point of view"): we see the drama through the eyes of Lockwood and Nelly Dean, who belong firmly to the world of practical reality. Sifted through the idiom of their commonplace vision, the drama taking place among the major characters finds contact with the temporal and the secular. Because Lockwood and Nelly Dean have witnessed the incredible violence of the life at the Heights, or rather, because Nelly Dean has witnessed the full span and capacity of that violence and because Lockwood credits her witness, the drama is oriented in the context of the psychologically familiar. There is also another technical bulwark that supports this uneasy tale in the social and moral imagination, and that is its extension over the lives of two generations and into a time of ameliorated and respectable manners. At the end, we see young Cathy teaching Hareton his letters and correcting his boorishness (which, after all, is only the natural boorishness consequent on neglect, and has none of the cannibal unregeneracy of Heathcliff in it); the prospect is one of decent, socially responsible domesticity. For this part of the tale, Lockwood alone is sufficient witness; and the fact that now Nelly Dean's experienced old eyes and memory can be dispensed with assures us of the present reasonableness and objectivity of events, and even infects retrospection on what has happened earlier— making it possible for the dream-rejecting reason to settle complacently for the "naturalness" of the entire story. If ghosts have been mentioned, if the country people swear that Heathcliff "walks," we can, with Lockwood at the end, affirm our skepticism as to "how anyone could ever imagine unquiet slumbers for the sleepers in that quiet earth."

Let us try to diagram these technical aspects of the work, for the compositional soundness of *Wuthering Heights* is owing to them. We may divide the action of the book into two parts, following each other chronologically, the one associated with the earlier generation (Hindley and Catherine and Heathcliff, Edgar and Isabella Linton), the other with the later generation (young Cathy and Linton and Hareton). The first of these actions is centered in what we shall call a "mythological romance"—for the astonishingly ravenous and possessive, perfectly amoral love of Cath-

erine and Heathcliff belongs to that realm of the imagination where myths
are created. The second action, centered in the protracted effects of Heathcliff's revenge, involves two sets of young lives and two small "romances":
the childish romance of Cathy and Linton, which Heathcliff manages to
pervert utterly; and the successful assertion of a healthy, culturally viable
kind of love between Cathy and Hareton, asserted as Heathcliff's cruel
energies flag and decay. Binding the two "actions" is the perduring figure
of Heathcliff himself, demon-lover in the first, paternal ogre in the second.
Binding them also is the framing narrational convention or "point of view":
the voices of Nelly Dean and Lockwood are always in our ears; one or the
other of them is always present at a scene, or is the confidant of someone
who was present; through Lockwood we encounter Heathcliff at the beginning of the book, and through his eyes we look on Heathcliff's grave
at the end. Still another pattern that binds the two actions is the repetition
of what we shall call the "two children" figure—two children raised virtually as brother and sister, in a vibrant relationship of charity and passion
and real or possible metamorphosis. The figure is repeated, with variation,
three times, in the relationships of the main characters. Of this we shall
speak again later. The technical continuities or patterning of the book could,
then, be simplified in this way:

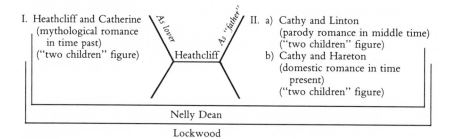

What, concretely, is the effect of this strict patterning and binding?
What does it "mean"? The design of the book is drawn in the spirit of
intense compositional rigor, of *limitation;* the characters act in the spirit of
passionate immodelacy, of *excess.* Let us consider this contrast a little more
closely. Essentially, *Wuthering Heights* exists for the mind as a tension between two kinds of reality: the raw, inhuman reality of anonymous natural
energies, and the restrictive reality of civilized habits, manners, and codes.
The first kind of reality is given to the imagination in the violent figures
of Catherine and Heathcliff, portions of the flux of nature, children of rock
and heath and tempest, striving to identify themselves as human, but dis-

rupting all around them with their monstrous appetite for an inhuman kind of intercourse, and finally disintegrated from within by the very energies out of which they are made. It is this vision of a reality radically alien from the human that the ancient Chinese landscape paintings offer also. But in those ancient paintings there is often a tiny human figure, a figure that is obviously that of a philosopher, for instance, or that of a peasant—in other words, a human figure decisively belonging to and representing a culture— who is placed in diminutive perspective beside the enormously cascading torrent, or who is seen driving his water buffalo through the overwhelming mists or faceless snows; and this figure is outlined sharply, so that, though it is extremely tiny, it is very definite in the giant surrounding indefiniteness. The effect is one of contrast between finite and infinite, between the limitation of the known and human, and the unlimitedness of the unknown and the nonhuman. So also in *Wuthering Heights:* set over against the wilderness of inhuman reality is the quietly secular, voluntarily limited, safely human reality that we find in the gossipy concourse of Nelly Dean and Lockwood, the one an old family servant with a strong grip on the necessary emotional economies that make life endurable, the other a city visitor in the country, a man whose very disinterestedness and facility of feeling and attention indicate the manifold emotional economies by which city people particularly protect themselves from any disturbing note of the ironic discord between civilized life and the insentient wild flux of nature in which it is islanded. This second kind of reality is given also in the romance of Cathy and Hareton, where book learning and gentled manners and domestic charities form a little island of complacence. The tension between these two kinds reality, their inveterate opposition and at the same time their *continuity* one with another, provides at once the content and the form of *Wuthering Heights.* We see the tension graphically in the diagram given above. The inhuman excess of Heathcliff's and Catherine's passion, an excess that is carried over into the second half of the book by Heathcliff's revenge, an excess everywhere present in language—in verbs and modifiers and metaphors that seethe with a brute fury—this excess is held within a most rigorous pattern of repeated motifs and of what someone has called the "Chinese box" of Nelly Dean's and Lockwood's interlocution. The form of the book, then—a form that may be expressed as a tension between the impulse to excess and the impulse to limitation or economy—*is* the content. The form, in short, is the book itself. Only in the fully wrought, fully realized, work of art does form so exhaust the possibilities of the material that it identifies itself with these possibilities.

If there has been any cogency in what we have said above, we should ask now how it is that the book is able to represent dramatically, in terms of human "character," its vision of the inhuman. After all, Catherine and Heathcliff *are* "characters," and not merely molecular vibrations in the primordial surge of things; indeed, they are so credibly characterized that Hollywood has been able to costume and cosmeticize them. As "characters," what are they? As lovers, what kind of love is theirs? They gnash and foam at each other. One could borrow for them a line from a poem by John Crowe Ransom describing lovers in hell: "Stuprate, they rend each other when they kiss." This is not "romantic love," as that term has popular meaning; and it is not even sexual love, naturalistically considered—the impulse to destruction is too pure in it, too simple and direct. Catherine says she *is* Heathcliff, and the implication is not of the possibility of a "mating," for one does not "mate" with oneself. Similarly, after her death, when Heathcliff howls that he cannot live without his *life,* he cannot live without his *soul* (and Nellie says that he "howled, not like a man, but like a savage beast"), the relationship and the destiny suggested are not those of adult human lovers, because the complex attendant motivations of adult life are lacking. But the emotional implications of Catherine's and Heathcliff's passion are never "adult," in the sense of there being in that passion any recognition of the domestic and social responsibilities, and the spiritual complexities, of adult life. Whatever could happen to these two, if they could be happily together, would be something altogether asocial, amoral, savagely irresponsible, wildly impulsive: it would be the enthusiastic, experimental, quite random activity of childhood, occult to the socialized adult. But since no conceivable *human* male and female, not brutish, not anthropologically rudimentary, could be together in this way as adults, all that we can really imagine for the grown-up Catherine and Heathcliff, as "characters" on the human plane, is what the book gives of them—their mutual destruction by tooth and nail in an effort, through death, to get back to the lost state of gypsy freedom in childhood.

Caught in the economical forms of adult life—concepts of social and intellectual "betterment" (such as lead Catherine to marry Edgar Linton), the frames of wealth and property ownership (which Heathcliff at first exploits in order to "raise" himself to Catherine's standard, and then as an engine of revenge against both the Earnshaws and the Lintons), marital relationships, and parenthood—they are, for the imagination, "humanized," endowed with "character," at least to the extent that we see their explosive confusions, resistances, and misery convulsing the forms usual to human adulthood. Their obsession, their prime passion, is also "human" although it is utterly destructive of the values signified by that word: the passion to lose the self in some "otherness," whether in complete identi-fication with another person (an identification for which "mating" is a surrogate only of a temporary and lapsing kind), or by absorption into "nature"—but it is a passion that is tabooed for the socialized adult, dis-guised, held in check by the complex cultural economies, safely stabled in the unconscious, at best put to work in that darkness to turn the mill of other objectives. This regressive passion is seen in uncompromised purity in Catherine and Heathcliff, and it opens the prospect of disintegration—disintegration into the unconsciousness of childhood and the molecular fluidity of death—in a word, into anonymous natural energy.

If the story of Catherine and Heathcliff had not been a story told by an old woman as something that had had its inception many years ago, if the old woman who tells the story had not been limited in imagination and provincial in her sympathies, if the story had been dramatized immediately in the here-and-now and not at a temporal remove and through a dispas-sioned intermediator, it is doubtful that it would resonate emotionally for us or carry any conviction—even any "meaning." Because of the very fact that the impulses it represents are taboo, they can conveniently be observed only at a remove, as someone else's, as of the past, and from the judicial point of view of conventional manners. The "someone else's" and the "long ago" are the mind's saving convention for making a distance with itself such as will allow it perspective. Thus the technical *displacement* of Heath-cliff's and Catherine's story into past time and into the memory of an old woman functions in the same way as dream displacements: it both censors and indulges, protects and liberates.

Significantly, our first real contact with the Catherine-Heathcliff drama is established through a dream—Lockwood's dream of the ghost-child at the window. Lockwood is motivated to dream the dream by the most easily convincing circumstances; he has fallen asleep while reading Catherine's diary, and during his sleep a tempest-blown branch is scratching on the windowpane. But why should Lockwood, the well-mannered urbanite, dream *this?*

> I pulled its wrist on to the broken pane, and rubbed it to and
> fro till the blood ran down and soaked the bedclothes.

The image is probably the most cruel one in the book. Hareton's hanging puppies, Heathcliff's hanging the springer spaniel, Hindley's forcing a knife between Nelly's teeth or throwing his baby over the staircase, Catherine's leaving the blue print of her nails on Isabella's arm, Heathcliff stamping on Hindley's face—these images and others like them imply savagery or revengefulness or drunkenness or hysteria, but always a motivating set of emotional circumstances. But this is the punctilious Lockwood—whose antecedents and psychology are so insipid that we care little about them—who scrapes the dream-waif's wrist back and forth on broken glass till the blood runs down and soaks the bedclothes. The cruelty of the dream is the gratuitousness of the violence wrought on a child by an emotionally un-motivated vacationer from the city, dreaming in a strange bed. The bed is an old-fashioned closet bed ("a large oak case . . . it formed a little closet" with a window set in it): its paneled sides Lockwood has "pulled together" before going to sleep. The bed is like a coffin (at the end of the book, Heathcliff dies in it, behind its closed panels); it had been Catherine's bed, and the movable panels themselves suggest the coffin in which she is laid, whose "panels" Heathcliff bribes the sexton to remove at one side. Psy-chologically, Lockwood's dream has only the most perfunctory determi-nations, and nothing at all of result for the dreamer himself, except to put him uncomfortably out of bed. But poetically the dream has its reasons, compacted into the image of the daemonic child scratching at the pane, trying to get from the "outside" "in," and of the dreamer in a bed like a coffin, released by that deathly privacy to indiscriminate violence. The coffin-like bed shuts off any interference with the wild deterioration of the psyche. Had the dream used any other agent then the effete, almost epicene Lockwood, it would have lost this symbolic force; for Lockwood, more successfully than anyone else in the book, has shut out the powers of darkness (the pun in his name is obvious in this context); and his lack of any dramatically thorough motivation for dreaming the cruel dream sug-gests those powers as existing autonomously, not only in the "outsideness" of external nature, beyond the physical windowpane, but also within, even in the soul least prone to passionate excursion.

The windowpane is the medium, treacherously transparent, separating the "inside" from the "outside," the "human" from the alien and terrible "other." Immediately after the incident of the dream, the time of the nar-rative is displaced into the childhood of Heathcliff and Catherine, and we see the two children looking through the window of the Linton's drawing room.

> "Both of us were able to look in by standing on the basement, and clinging to the ledge, and we saw—ah! it was beautiful—a splendid place carpeted with crimson, and crimson-covered chairs and tables, and a pure white ceiling bordered by gold, a shower of glass-drops hanging in silver chains from the centre,

and shimmering with little soft tapers. Old Mr. and Mrs. Linton were not there; Edgar and his sister had it entirely to themselves. Shouldn't they have been happy? We should have thought ourselves in heaven!"

Here the two unregenerate waifs look *in* from the night on the heavenly vision of the refinements and securities of the most privileged human estate. But Heathcliff rejects the vision: seeing the Linton children blubbering and bored there (*they* cannot get *out!*), he senses the menace of its limitations; while Catherine is fatally tempted. She is taken in by the Lintons, and now it is Heathcliff alone outside looking through the window.

"The curtains were still looped up at one corner, and I resumed my station as a spy; because Catherine had wished to return, I intended shattering their great glass panes to a million of fragments, unless they let her out. She sat on the sofa quietly . . . the woman-servant brought a basin of warm water, and washed her feet; and Mr. Linton mixed a tumbler of negus, and Isabella emptied a plateful of cakes into her lap . . . Afterwards, they dried and combed her beautiful hair."

Thus the first snare is laid by which Catherine will be held for a human destiny—her feet washed, cakes and wine for her delectation, her beautiful hair combed (the motifs here are limpid as those of fairy tale, where the changeling in the "otherworld" is held there mysteriously by bathing and by the strange new food he has been given to eat). By her marriage to Edgar Linton, Catherine yields to that destiny; later she resists it tormentedly and finds her way out of it by death. Literally she "catches her death" by throwing open the window.

"Open the window again wide: fasten it open! Quick, why don't you move?" [she says to Nelly].
"Because I won't give you your death of cold," I answered.
"You won't give me a chance of life, you mean," she said.

In her delirium, she opens the window, leans out into the winter wind, and calls across the moors to Heathcliff,

"Heathcliff, if I dare you now, will you venture . . . Find a way, then! . . . You are slow! . . . you always followed me!"

On the night after her burial, unable to follow her (though he digs up her grave in order to lie beside her in the coffin from which the side panels have been removed), he returns to the Heights *through the window*—for

Hindley has barred the door—to wreak on the living the fury of his frustration. It is years later that Lockwood arrives at the Heights and spends his uncomfortable night there. Lockwood's outcry in his dream brings Heathcliff *to the window,* Heathcliff who has been caught ineluctably in the human to grapple with its interdictions long after Catherine has broken through them. The treachery of the window is that Catherine, lost now in the "other," can look through the transparent membrane that separates her from humanity, can scratch on the pane, but cannot get "in," while Heathcliff, though he forces the window open and howls into the night, cannot get "out." When he dies, Nelly Dean discovers the window swinging open, the window of that old-fashioned coffin-like bed where Lockwood had had the dream. Rain has been pouring in during the night, drenching the dead man. Nelly says,

> I hasped the window; I combed his black long hair from his forehead; I tried to close his eyes: to extinguish, if possible, that frightful, lifelike gaze of exultation before any one else beheld it. They would not shut: they seemed to sneer at my attempts.

Earlier, Heathcliff's eyes have been spoken of as "the clouded windows of hell" from which a "fiend" looks out. All the other uses of the "window" that we have spoken of here are not figurative but perfectly naturalistic uses, though their symbolic value is inescapable. But the fact that Heathcliff's eyes refuse to close in death suggests the symbol in a metaphorical form (the "fiend" has now got "out," leaving the window open), elucidating with simplicity the meaning of the "window" as a separation between the daemonic depths of the soul and the limited and limiting lucidities of consciousness, a separation between the soul's "otherness" and its humanness.

There is still the difficulty of defining, with any precision, the quality of the daemonic that is realized most vividly in the conception of Heathcliff, a difficulty that is mainly due to our tendency always to give the "daemonic" some ethical status—that is, to relate it to an ethical hierarchy. Heathcliff's is an archetypal figure, untraceably ancient in mythological thought—an imaged recognition of that part of nature which is "other" than the human soul (the world of the elements and the animals) and of that part of the soul itself which is "other" than the conscious part. But since Martin Luther's revival of this archetype for modern mythology, it has tended to forget its relationship with the elemental "otherness" of the outer world and to identify itself solely with the dark functions of the soul. As an image of soul work, it is ethically relevant, since everything that the soul does—even unconsciously, even "ignorantly" (as in the case of Oedipus)—offers itself for ethical judgment, whereas the elements and the animals do not. Puritanism perpetuated the figure for the imagination; Milton give it its greatest aesthetic splendor, in the fallen angel through whom the divine beauty still shone; Richardson introduced it, in the person of Lovelace, to an infatuated middle class; and always the figure was ethically relevant through the conception of "sin" and "guilt." (Let us note here, however, the ambivalence of the figure, an ambivalence that the medieval devil does not have. The medieval devil a really ugly customer, so ugly that he can even become a comedy figure—as in the medieval moralities. The daemonic archetype of which we are speaking here is deeply serious in quality because of his ambivalence: he is a fertilizing energy and profoundly attractive, and at the same time horribly destructive to civilized institutionalism. It is because of his ambivalence that, though he is the "enemy," ethically speaking, he so easily takes on the stature and beauty of a hero, as he does in the Satan of *Paradise Lost*.) In Byron's *Manfred*, the archetype underwent a rather confusing sea-change, for Manfred's crime is, presumably, so frightful that it cannot be mentioned, and the indefinable nature of the crime blurs the edges of the figure and cuts down its resonance in the imagination (when we guess that the crime might be incest, we are disposed to find this a rather paltry equation for the Byronic incantation of guilt); nevertheless, the ethical relevancy of the figure remains. Let us follow it a little further, before returning to Emily Brontë's Heathcliff. In the later nineteenth century, in the novels of Dostoyevski, it reappears with an enormous development of psychological subtlety, and also with a great strengthening and clarification of its ethical significance. In the work of André Gide, it undergoes another sea-change: the archetypal daemonic figure now becomes the principle of progress, the spirit of free investigation and creative experience; with this reorientation, it becomes positively ethical rather than negatively so. In Thomas Mann's *Doctor Faustus*, it reverts to its earlier and more constant significance, as the type of the instinctive part of the soul, a great and fertilizing power, but ethically unregenerate and therefore a great danger to ethical man.

Our interest in sketching some phases of the history of this archetype has been to show that it has had, in modern mythology, constantly a status in relation to ethical thought. The exception is Heathcliff. Heathcliff is no more ethically relevant than is flood or earthquake or whirlwind. It is as impossible to speak of him in terms of "sin" and "guilt" as it is to speak in this way of the natural elements or the creatures of the animal world. In him, the type reverts to a more ancient mythology and to an earlier symbolism. *Wuthering Heights* so baffles and confounds the ethical sense because it is not informed with that sense at all: it is profoundly informed with the attitudes of "animism," by which the natural world—that world which is "other" than and "outside of" the consciously individualized human—*appears* to act with an energy similar to the energies of the soul; to be permeated with soul energy but of a mysterious and alien kind that the conscious human soul, bent on securing itself through civilization, cannot identify itself with as to purpose; an energy that can be propitiated, that can at times be canalized into humanly purposeful channels, that *must* be given religious recognition both for its enormous fertility and its enormous potential destructiveness. But Heathcliff does have human shape and human relationships; he is, so to speak, "caught in" the human; two kinds of reality intersect in him—as they do, with a somewhat different balance, in Catherine; as they do, indeed, in the other characters. Each entertains, in some degree, the powers of darkness—from Hindley, with his passion for self-destruction (he, too, wants to get "out"), to Nelly Dean, who in a sense "propitiates" those powers with the casuistry of her actions, and even to Lockwood, with his sadistic dream. Even in the weakest of these souls there is an intimation of the dark Otherness, by which the soul is related psychologically to the inhuman world of pure energy, for it carries within itself an "otherness" of its own, that inhabits below consciousness.

The imagery of the windowpane is metamorphic, suggesting a total change of mode of being by the breaking-through of a separating medium that exists between consciousness and the "other." The strangest and boldest and most radiant figuration that Emily Brontë has given to her subject is the "two children" figure, also a metamorphic figure of breakthrough and transformation. The *type* or classic form of this figure is a girl with golden hair and a boy with dark hair and shadowed brow, bound in kinship and in a relationship of charity and passion, and with a metamorphosis of some kind potential in the relationship. The beautiful dark boy will be brightened, made angelic and happy, by the beautiful golden girl: this, apparently, is what *should* happen. But the dynamics of the change are not perfectly trustworthy. In one of Emily Brontë's poems, describing a child who might be the child Heathcliff, the ambivalent dark boy will evidently sink further into his darkness.

> I love thee, boy; for all divine,
> All full of God thy features shine.
> Darling enthusiast, holy child,
> Too good for this world's warring wild,
> Too heavenly now but doomed to be
> Hell-like in heart and misery.

In the 1850 printing of the Brontë poems (the printing supervised by the Brontë sisters) two companion pieces appear under the title "The Two Children," in the first of which the dark boy is still unchanged.

> Frowning on the infant,
> Shadowing childhood's joy,
> Guardian angel knows not
> That melancholy boy.

In the second of these companion pieces, the golden child is evoked, and now the change in the dark one is promised.

> Child of Delight! with sunbright hair,
> And seablue, seadeep eyes;
> Spirit of Bliss, what brings thee here,
> Beneath these sullen skies?
>
> Though shouldest live in eternal spring,
> Where endless day is never dim;
> Why, Seraph, has thy erring wing
> Borne thee down to weep with him?

She answers that she is "not from heaven descended," but that she has seen and pities "that mournful boy."

> And I swore to take his gloomy sadness,
> And give to him my beamy joy.

Here, with the change of the dark child, the golden child will be changed also, for she will take his "gloomy sadness." In another set of verses, the light-dark contrast is turned around bewilderingly.

> And only *he* had locks of light,
> And *she* had raven hair;
> While now, his curls are dark as night,
> And hers as morning fair.

What really seems to be implied by all these shifts is not a mere exchange of characteristics but a radical identification of the two children, so that each can appear in the mode of the other, the bright one in the mode of darkness and the dark one in the mode of light.

In still another of those poems that dramatize affairs in the kingdom of Gondal that occupied Emily Brontë's youthful fantasy, a brooding phantom figure haunts the moonlit grounds of a castle. Its face is "divinely fair," but on its "angel brow"

> Rests such a shade of deep despair
> As nought divine could ever know.

Apparently the cause of his death was adoration of another man's wife ("Lord Alfred's idol queen"), and it is for this reason that his spirit is "shut from heaven—an outcast for eternity." The woman for whom he died is represented as an "infant fair," looking from a golden frame in a portrait gallery.

> And just like his its ringlets bright,
> Its large dark eye of shadowy light,
> Its cheeks' pure hue, its forehead white,
> And like its noble name.

A deliberate confusion of the planes of reality—a sifting into the life inside the picture frame (like the shifts "through the window" in *Wuthering Heights*), and with it a shifting from despairing adulthood into childhood—is suggested with the following questions:

> And did he never smile to see
> Himself restored to infancy?
>
> Never part back that golden flow
> Of curls, and kiss that pearly brow,
> And feel no other earthly bliss
> Was equal to that parent's kiss?

The suggestions are those of metamorphic changes, but all under the aspect of frustration: the despairing lover cannot get through the picture frame where the child is. Other motifs here are reminiscent of those of *Wuthering Heights*. The spectral lover is an ambivalent figure, of divine beauty, but an outcast from heaven. Kinship is suggested between him and the child in the picture ("And just like his its ringlets bright . . . And like its noble name"), and one is left to imagine that "Lord Alfred's idol queen" was his sister, wherefore the frustration of their love. The last stanza quoted above remarks ambiguously on the parental feeling involved in the relationship: is it not the infant who is the "parent" here? Parental charity is the feeling of the golden "guardian angel" for her dark charge in "The Two Children" poems, as it is, in a degree, of Catherine for Heathcliff during their childhood, and of young Cathy first for Linton and then for Hareton. The fact that, in the poem, both the infant and the spectral lover have golden hair seems, in this elusive fantasy, to be a mark of perversion of the metamorphic sequence, at least of its having gone awry (as in the case, too, of young Cathy and Linton, who is not dark but fair).

In the relationship of Catherine and Heathcliff, the fantasy has its typical form. She is golden, he is dark. His daemonic origin is always kept open, by reiterations of the likelihood that he is really a ghoul, a fiend, an offspring of hell, and not merely so in behavior. And Catherine also, like the guardian child in "The Two Children" poems, is "not from heaven descended": she has furious tantrums, she lies, she bites, her chosen toy is a whip. They are raised as brother and sister; there are three references to their sleeping in the same bed as infants. She scolds and orders and mothers and cherishes him ("much too fond of him" as a child, Nelly says). The notions of somatic change and discovery of noble birth, as in fairy tale, are deliberately played with; as, when Catherine returns from her first sojourn at the Lintons' and Heathcliff asks Nelly to "make him decent," he says, comparing himself with Edgar,

> "I wish I had light hair and a fair skin, and was dressed and behaved as well, and had a chance of being as rich as he will be!"

and Nelly answers,

> "You're fit for a prince in disguise . . . Were I in your place, I would frame high notions of my birth."

(If Heathcliff is really of daemonic origin, he is, in a sense, indeed of "high birth," a "prince in disguise," and might be expected, like the princes of fairy tale, to drop his "disguise" at the crisis of the tale and be revealed in original splendor: the dynamics of the "two children" figure also points to the potential transformation.) Some alluring and astonishing destiny seems possible for the two. *What* that phenomenon might be or mean, we cannot know, for it is frustrated by Catherine's marriage to Edgar, which dooms Heathcliff to be "hell-like in heart and misery." Catherine's decision dooms her also, for she is of the same daemonic substance as Heathcliff, and a civilized marriage and domesticity are not sympathetic to the daemonic quality.

With the second generation, the "two children" figure is distorted and parodied in the relationship of Catherine's daughter and Heathcliff's son. Young Cathy, another "child of delight, with sunbright hair," has still some of the original daemonic energy, but her "erring wing" has brought her down to "weep with" a *pale-haired* and pallid little boy whose only talents are for sucking sugar candy and torturing cats. She does her best, as infant mother, to metamorphose him, but he is an ungrateful and impossible subject. Her passionate charity finally finds her "married" to his corpse in a locked bedroom. With Cathy and Hareton Earnshaw, her cousin on her mother's side, the "two children" are again in their right relationship of golden and dark, and now the pathos of the dark child cures the daemon out of the golden one, and the maternal care of the golden child raises the dark one to civilized humanity and makes of him a proper husband.

In these several pairs, the relation of kinship has various resonances. Between Catherine and Heathcliff, identity of "kind" is greatest, although they are foster brother and sister only. The foster kinship provides an imaginative implicit reason for the unnaturalness and impossibility of their mating. Impassioned by their brother-and-sisterlike identity of kind, they can only destroy each other, for it is impossible for two persons to *be* each other (as Catherine says she "is" Heathcliff) without destruction of the physical limitations that individualize and separate. In Emily Brontë's use of the symbolism of the incest motive, the incestual impulse appears as an attempt to make what is "outside" oneself identical with what is "inside" oneself—a performance that can be construed in physical and human terms only by violent destruction of personality bounds, by rending of flesh and at last by death.

With Catherine's daughter and young Linton, who are cousins, the implicit incestuousness of the "two children" figure is suggested morbidly by Linton's disease and by his finally becoming a husband only as a corpse. With Cathy and Hareton Earnshaw, also cousins, Victorian "ameliorism" finds a way to sanction the relationship by symbolic emasculation; Cathy literally teaches the devil out of Hareton, and "esteem" between the two takes the place of the old passion for identification. With this successful metamorphosis and mating, the daemonic quality has been completely suppressed, and, though humanity and civilization have been secured for the "two children," one feels that some magnificent bounty is now irrecoverable. The great magic, the wild power, of the original two has been lost.

We are led to speculate on what the bounty might have been, had the windowpane not stood between the original pair, had the golden child and the dark child not been secularized by a spelling book. Perhaps, had the ideal and impossible eventuality taken place, had the "inside" and the "outside," the bright child and the dark one, become identified in such a way that they could freely assume each other's modes, then perhaps the world of the animals and the elements—the world of wild moor and barren rock, of fierce wind and attacking beast, that is the strongest palpability in *Wuthering Heights*—would have offered itself completely to human understanding and creative intercourse. Perhaps the dark powers that exist within the soul, as well as in the outer elemental world, would have assumed the language of consciousness, or consciousness would have bravely entered into companionship with those dark powers and transliterated their language into its own. Emily Brontë's book has been said to be nonphilosophical—as it is certainly nonethical; but all philosophy is not ethics, and the book seizes, at the point where the soul feels itself cleft within and in cleavage from the universe, the first germs of philosophic thought, the thought of the duality of human and nonhuman existence, and the thought of the cognate duality of the psyche.

Wuthering Heights and the Limits of Vision

David Sonstroem

Wuthering Heights tends to be read for its purple passions—read as though those passions and the rationale behind them were being endorsed by Emily Brontë. But such a reading does not do the novel full justice. It does not treat an important element in the actual page-by-page experience of reading, namely, the uneasiness or confusion of the reader: his vacillating allegiances, his sense of being afloat on a troubled conceptual and ethical sea. Much of the reader's confusion is due to the pervasive and obvious shortsightedness of all the characters, incuding Heathcliff and Catherine. The somewhat Lawrencian outlook that the two leading figures harbor at the base of their natures but only partly understand simply does not take the whole world of *Wuthering Heights* into comprehensive account. In fact their shortsightedness is very similar in kind to that of everyone else. I wish to argue that *Wuthering Heights* presents the spectacle of several limited and inadequate points of view—genteel, Christian, pragmatic, animistic—at indecisive war with one another. Far from wholeheartedly endorsing an order, Emily Brontë depicts conceptual wuthering. She addresses herself less to vision than to blindness: to man's refusal to overlook his prejudices, and his inability to discern what lies beyond his limitations.

The general failure to understand one another is frequently and simply revealed by means of what might be called the "nowt"-device of perceptual censorship. Joseph is ever calling everyone else a "nowt," a nothing, denying everyone a place (except in hell) in his scheme of things: "Bud yah're

From *PMLA* 86, no. 1 (January 1971). © 1971 by The Modern Language Association of America.

a nowt, . . . like yer mother afore ye!"; "marred, wearisome nowt"; "gooid fur nowt, slattenly witch"; "nasty, ill nowt." Joseph's "nowt" is only the most humorous and inconsequential outcropping of disregard, for others are just as adept as he at wishing away. The many lockings-out are a general expression of the cognitive deletion, and the Earnshaw family's reaction to Heathcliff upon his first introduction is the best communal example: Mrs. Earnshaw "was ready to fling it out of doors"; Catherine and Hindley "entirely refused to have it in bed with them, or even in their room"; and Nelly "put it on the landing of the stairs, hoping it might be gone on the morrow."

All the characters demonstrate such denial. Nelly Dean's characteristic "Hush" and "Wisht" show how basic denial is to her outlook. Her utterances are filled with such expressions as "nothing," "nonsense," "worthless trash," and "I won't hear it!" And Edgar is another denier. Like Nelly, he calls Heathcliff "worthless." He tries unsuccessfully to ban him from the Grange and then from the mind of his wife. Later he tries unsuccessfully to withhold all knowledge of Wuthering Heights from his daughter. He tries, moreover, to wish away not only Heathcliff but his own sister: "Trouble me no more about her"; "I have nothing to forgive her, Ellen. . . . My communication with Heathcliff's family shall be as sparing as his with mine. It shall not exist!"

Less important characters also engage in disregard, giving the reader the sense that "It shall not exist!" is the sentiment of all. Old Mr. Earnshaw remarks, "Hindley was naught, and would never thrive as where he wandered." When Hindley sets out upon a reckless, dissipated life after his wife's death, "The curate dropped calling, and nobody decent came near us." Hindley himself tries to keep Hareton out of his sight, as he had the young Heathcliff. Isabella "would that [Heathcliff] could be blotted out of creation, and out of my memory." When Cathy Linton pleads for help for her dying husband, Zillah feels that "it was no concern of mine." On a happier note, the course of Cathy Linton's second romance depends upon her overcoming her tendency to disregard Hareton: "I never missed such a concern as you." "What a blank dreary mind he must have!" And Hareton must recognize his own extra-animal feelings of love as something other than "naught, naught."

Taken individually, such passages often indicate nothing more than antipathy or disagreement. But the fact that the same mode for expressing disagreement is employed so frequently by so many characters suggests a further significance—suggests, in fact, a partial explanation for the many antipathies. How one feels is related to how one sees. The pervasiveness of the "nowt"-device reveals that the principal disagreements in the novel are not what might be termed honest ones, which come about after a full examination and appreciation of another's position. They are revealed to be rather the result of a general impulse to ignore someone or something disagreeable by averting one's eyes. In this way *Wuthering Heights* presents the concept of limited vision as a part of its complex of concerns.

But the "nowt"-device is just one motif or structural principle by which the shortsightedness of the characters is established. The limitations of vision are not all so negative, so culpable, for often a character is unable to understand and appreciate, even when he earnestly desires to do so. The broadest indications of perceptual shortcomings are the many betrayed expectations. *Wuthering Heights* is a book of best-laid plans gone awry: Mr. Earnshaw's hopes at introducing Heathcliff to his family; Catherine Earnshaw's hopes for her marriage to Edgar; Edgar's expectations that he can shield his daughter from the outside world, and, later, that he can bring her happiness by encouraging a marriage between her and Linton; Nelly's silly wish that Lockwood will marry Cathy Linton; Heathcliff's "violent exertions" for revenge that come to an "absurd termination." The novel is full of "absurd terminations."

Allan R. Brick has pointed out how Lockwood's preconceptions, based on his genteel, bookish background and conventionally romantic cast, are serially betrayed when he tries to use them to make sense of the actual state of affairs at Wuthering Heights. Lockwood discovers an "amiable hostess" who does not respond to small talk, a nest of cats that is really a heap of dead rabbits: "Intrepidly, Lockwood rattles off one misinterpretation after another about the identity of the people in Wuthering Heights and their (he presumes) normal relations with each other. . . . Finally he comes to a dim awareness, if not an admission that he has stepped into a land and a dwelling . . . where none of his mundane methods of perception will apply." Brick goes on to remark that "Lockwood's inability to make out the inside of Wuthering Heights is matched by his puzzled scrutiny of its exterior, where the landmarks and dangerous pitfalls have been concealed by snow." This image of a man floundering in a world of obliterated landmarks has its application well beyond Lockwood.

For example, Cathy Linton also receives a conceptual shock at Wuthering Heights. Her newfound friend Hareton does not fit her familiar categories of master's son or master's servant. And she refuses to accept the boor as her "cousin," that term being reserved for the "gentleman's son," Linton. She is further upset by Hareton's calling her a "damned . . . saucy witch" instead of "Miss" or "angel." Her adventure might be said to be semantic as well as social, and her little, sheltered world more injured by it than were her pampered dogs. And Isabella, too, has trouble adjusting her world to the Heights—trouble indicated through her inability to comprehend the organization of rooms:

> "Have you no place you call a parlour?"
> "*Parlour!*" [Joseph] echoed, sneeringly, "*parlour!* Nay, we've noa *parlours.*"

And again:

> "Why, man!" I exclaimed, facing him angrily, "this is not a place to sleep in. I wish to see my bed-room."
> "*Bed-rume!*" he repeated, in a tone of mockery. "Yah's see all t' *bed-rumes* thear is."

She wanders helplessly through the house, her conventional expectations failing utterly to guide her. (With her plight here, compare Heathcliff at the Grange: "He did not hit the right room directly.")

In a larger sense, Christianity serves as a motif employed to expose the conceptual inadequacies of a whole community. The parson will not come till morning, and the curate, not at all; Gimmerton Chapel is in a more advanced decay than the peat-embalmed bodies beneath it; God prevents no atrocities, punishes no sinners. Fanatic Joseph, whose greatest function seems to be personifying the total irrelevance and unimportance of fire-breathing evangelicalism to the workings of the world of *Wuthering Heights,* is loudly impotent. When Nelly Dean sermonizes to Heathcliff, just before his death, upon his unchristian life, his unfamiliarity with the Bible, and his need for "some minister of any denomination," we feel that, despite her bland ecumenicity, she is being impertinent, in all senses of the word. As an operative force, Christianity is at best invisible to mortal eye, and as theory, transformed into ranting or canting by its professors. It serves in the novel as the most conspicuous example of a schema that fails to do justice to things as they are.

Although the pagan Heathcliff and his Catherine gain a certain sympathy from the reader because of the incomprehension and exclusion directed against them by the other characters, they are as blind to aspects of the actual as are the others. For example, they employ the "nowt"-device like everyone else. To Heathcliff, Edgar is "the cipher at the Grange." He discounts Edgar's very real love for Catherine ("he couldn't love as much in eighty years as I could in a day"); and her love for Edgar ("He is scarcely a degree dearer to her than her dog, or her horse.") His own son is a "pitiful, shuffling, worthless thing." "His life is not worth a farthing." "Let me never hear a word more about him!" Of Cathy Linton—a "worthless bitch"—he declares, "I earnestly wish she were invisible." And he remarks, of Hareton and her, "if I could do it without seeming insane, I'd never see him again! . . . I can give them no attention any more." His exclusive proclivities also show themselves in his destruction of books: As a child, with Catherine, he destroys Joseph's oppressive tomes; as an adult, he destroys Cathy Linton's little library.

Like Heathcliff, Catherine Earnshaw is exclusive, but in an entirely involuntary and more painful way. When she declares her bond with Heathcliff we believe her: "If all else perished, and *he* remained, I should still continue to be; and if all else remained, and he were annihilated, the Universe would turn to a mighty stranger." But she does not explore the possibility that Heathcliff *and* "all else," including Edgar, might exist simultaneously. Characteristically, in spite of her best intentions, she disregards one or the other. It is very like her, at the Christmas party with the Linton children, to forget Heathcliff and his banishment for a time, only to remember and seek him out, now forgetting her guests. After her marriage, as long as Heathcliff stays away, Catherine can get along tolerably pleasantly; only in her Heathcliff phase does she call this time "bitter misery." But as soon as Heathcliff returns, it is Edgar who disappears before her eyes, or who unaccountably and annoyingly will *not* disappear. Earlier she had seen herself joined to Heathcliff while "every Linton on the face of the earth might melt into nothing." In her delirious fit, "the whole last seven years of my life"—the years since meeting Edgar—"grew a blank! I did not recall that they had been at all." And Edgar, standing before her, "was invisible to her abstracted gaze." Divided against herself, Catherine characteristically denies or disregards one aspect of herself. In spite of her desires for harmony, she is no more reconciled with herself than Heathcliff is united with Edgar. If her clinging to Heathcliff just before her death indicates a resolute decision, there is not much triumph in it, because it involves an exclusive choice rather than the comprehensive union that she sought throughout life.

Futhermore, the Heathcliff that she chooses is not even Heathcliff as he is: "Oh, you see, Nelly! he would not relent a moment, to keep me out of the grave! *That* is how I am loved! Well, never mind! That is not *my* Heathcliff. I shall love mine yet; and take him with me—he's in my soul." *Her* Heathcliff is purged of ugly traits, such as cruelty, relentlessness, and contrariety, that are indelibly a part of the actual Heathcliff's nature, as well as her own.

Heathcliff and Catherine are also like the other characters in that their shortsightedness does not always take the form of cognitive exclusion. For example, in the scene in which Lockwood misconstrues everything in sight, Heathcliff also has his genuine conceptual difficulties. There is some malicious joy in Heathcliff's forbidding Lockwood to spend the night in the sitting room, but there is also ignorance of the ways of civilized men, like Lockwood, against whom one need not be constantly on guard. During Lockwood's earlier visit, Heathcliff means to insult in saying that the dogs "won't meddle with persons who touch nothing"; but the remark also shows his ignorance of such subtler effrontery as Lockwood actually has practiced against the dogs, as well as his incomprehension of men so well-to-do and satisfied that unguarded goods offer no temptation to them. Heathcliff's view of things, along with Catherine's, is also shown to be inadequate in the scene in which they vie with each other in choosing the meanest animal—"lamb," "sucking leveret"—to suggest the cowardly, quivering nature of Linton. But Nelly implies that Edgar's trembling is due to strong emotions in a weak frame rather than to cowardice. And Edgar gives the lie to the epithets by rising up and striking Heathcliff "a blow that would have levelled a slighter man." He momentarily defeats Heathcliff on the latter's own, animal terms, overturning Heathcliff's and Catherine's expectations of him, and probably our own as well.

Heathcliff's greatest confusions are revealed in his attempts to deal with painful events by repeating or reliving them on more acceptable terms. The present always proves intractable to him, showing itself more complicated than his comprehension of it. Time will not oblige him by doubling back on itself. He runs away for three years to gain the polish needed to make Catherine choose him over Edgar, but when he returns, everything else has changed as well as himself. Although he knows even before his return that Catherine has married, he does not seem able to change tactics or to adjust to the new circumstances. After Catherine's death, he attempts to relive the past (adjusted to his desires) vicariously, through his son. According to his schema, Linton, his son, is to be Heathcliff-become-Edgar; Hareton, Hindley's son, is to be Hindley-become-Heathcliff; Cathy Linton, Catherine Earnshaw's daughter, is to be the new Catherine Earnshaw. But Heathcliff's alter ego Linton proves to have too much of his mother in him—too much "Linton"—to make identification possible. Hareton proves to be too attractive—too reminiscent of Heathcliff's own old self—to make vicarious animosity possible. And Cathy Linton, like her mother, is too attached to Edgar and his values for Heathcliff's satisfaction. Even before Linton dies, then, Heathcliff's hope of replaying his life on his own terms has collapsed. Once again, as when his return to Catherine proves fruitless,

he is offered only the substitute satisfaction of revenge rather than fulfillment. To this end, he holds in his power a child of each of his enemies on
whom to gain his revenge. But the children prove to be replicas—rather
faded ones—of his boyhood self and of Catherine. In the general neutral-
ization of impulses, Heathcliff loses interest in his immediate surroundings
and welcomes Catherine's apparition. His repeated failure to take a child's
"other" parent or guardian into account indicates systematically his inability
to cope with the present, to take all into account.

In these ways Emily Brontë insists upon the relativity and shortcomings
of all her characters' perceptions, including those of Heathcliff and Catherine. For all the windows and books in the novel, no one sees very far or
learns very much. Thrushcross Grange and Wuthering Heights are appropriately out of sight of one another. Ignorance does not lead to untroubled,
self-sufficient bliss, however. The "nowt"-device is not so successful nor
ignorance so complete that anyone in the book can finally close his doors
and windows to the world and its other inhabitants. But no one can accommodate them either. The characters' opinions and concepts, which
follow from their limited vision, run abrasively afoul of each other. There
is, however, no conceptual development as a result of the conflicts, no
sharpening of the better argument upon the dull stone of the worse. Instead,
the crossing of concepts dramatizes a general perceptual and epistemological
incompetence. No one is enlightened, and the reader is not drawn to endorse
anyone's views.

Lockwood's dream of the "Pious Discourse" of the Reverend Jabes
Branderham, with its multiple recriminations, typifies the larger conceptual
struggles in the novel. Branderham's four-hundred-ninety categories of sin
parody the other characters' attempts at ordering events. His tedious, arbitrary organization gives way abruptly upon the "First of the Seventy-
First," as order explodes into the violent confusion of mutual accusation.
(All charges in the novel are met by charges in return.) The question that
Branderham poses, namely, the nature of the unforgivable sin, is finally
beyond man's powers to answer satisfactorily. Neither he nor Lockwood
has reason to be so emphatically certain of his own conclusions. Yet each
grips a limited truth: Lockwood *has* been frivolous and inattentive; Branderham *has* been outrageously wearisome. According to his own dim lights,
each is justified; so each lays on with his own measuring stick upon the
other's shoulders. The result is a melee of limited, self-righteous partisans,
as "every man's hand was against his neighbour." Our sympathies are
largely with Lockwood here—his description of his distress touches our
tactile sense—but we do not really settle who (if anybody) is right.

Ordinarily the conceptual clashes are merely glancing, verbal ones.

Catherine Earnshaw frets at what she calls Nelly's "apathy," but Nelly takes pride in that emotional cast, calling it "stolidity." Neither word is really just: Nelly does have feelings, but she is too spineless and spiteful to be described as stolid. Later, when Nelly refuses to open a window, "because I won't give you your death of cold," Catherine contradicts her: "You won't give me a chance of life, you mean." In fact both agree on the projected result: Catherine would perish. Their real difference is over values: Nelly would preserve life at all costs, whereas Catherine would sacrifice a long life of confinement for a brief psychic contact with "what had been my world." Our sympathies for the suffering Catherine and the limitations of Nelly's too comfortable remark should not obscure the valid view in that remark. Again, Catherine, going to make her peace with Edgar, remarks, "I'm an angel!" But Nelly sees only "self-complacent conviction" in her gesture. One is flushed with self-congratulation at the prospect of domestic martyrdom; the other is thick-skinned and peevish. The reader is also aware that "angel" takes on the special aroma of the Linton family throughout the events of the book. Both of their verdicts need qualification.

Catherine Earnshaw and Nelly are not the only two who put different constructions upon the same events. The second Catherine and Linton engage in a naive quarrel of half-truths and oversimplifications, which reflect the biases of their respective fathers:

> Linton denied that people ever hated their wives; but Cathy affirmed they did, and in her wisdom, instanced his own father's aversion to her aunt. . . . "Papa told me; and papa does not tell falsehoods!" . . .
>
> "My papa scorns yours!" cried Linton. "He calls him a sneaking fool!"
>
> "Yours is a wicked man, . . . He must be wicked, to have made Aunt Isabella leave him as she did!" . . .
>
> "Well, I'll tell *you* something!" said Linton. "Your mother hated your father, now then. . . . And she loved mine!"

We feel their incompetence, their inability to understand fully the past of their families. Nor can they judge rightly or agree on an interpretation of their own experiences. After a fracas brought on mutually by Linton's infantile crankiness, Hareton's crude, short-tempered efforts to please Cathy, and Cathy's snobbery, she is "confounded" to hear Linton "utter the falsehood that I had occasioned the uproar, and Hareton was not to blame!"

Even the very compatible narrators occasionally manage to cancel each others' platitudes: Lockwood feels that the Gimmerton natives "*do* live more in earnest, more in themselves, and less in surface change, and frivolous external things." Nelly replies, "Oh! here we are the same as anywhere else, when you get to know us." The contrary opinions, neither entirely satisfactory, neutralize each other.

A more sustained example of crossed concepts involves explaining the nature of Heathcliff. He bursts into the world of Wuthering Heights as a marvel, a nova, sui generis, unsettling the other characters, who try futilely thereafter to fit him into their preexistent categories. Isabella writes Nelly, "Is Mr. Heathcliff a man? If so, is he mad? And if not, is he a devil?" Later she calls him a "monster," but Nelly answers, "Hush, hush! He's a human being. Be more charitable; there are worse men than he is yet!" But Isabella retorts, "He's not a human being," and Nelly herself has a few later doubts:

> "Is he a ghoul, or a vampire?" I mused. . . . And then I set myself to reflect how I had tended him in infancy; . . . and followed him almost through his whole course; and what absurd nonsense it was to yield to that sense of horror.
>
> "But where did he come from, the little dark thing, harboured by a good man to his bane?"

Is Heathcliff really only a foreigner: a "gipsy," "a little Lascar, or an American or Spanish castaway"? Is he a "prince in disguise"? Is he rather low-class: a "vulgar young ruffian," a "servant"? Is he a beast of prey in human form: "a fierce, pitiless, wolfish man"? Or is he an infernal, supernatural creature: a "devil," "goblin," "ghoul," or "vampire"? Is Nelly right in attributing his aberrations to a touch of madness: "He might have had a monomania on the subject of his departed idol; but on every other point his wits were as sound as mine"? Or is she closer to the truth in saying, "I did not feel as if I were in the company of a creature of my own species"? None of these doors to understanding is ever really closed; but none opens wide enough to let the whole Heathcliff through.

The concept of heaven provides further grounds for inconclusive disagreement. Except for Catherine Earnshaw's sadly inappropriate notion of heaven as the Grange, as marriage to Edgar—a heaven incompatible with her basic nature—each person's heaven is composed of those qualities that are most appealing to him; so there are as many heavens implied in the novel as there are points of view. Linton's heaven is a sleepy "ecstasy of peace"; the second Cathy's is "the whole world awake and wild with joy." Nelly Dean's "heterodox" heaven is, like herself, "untroubled," "shadowless," dull, and uniformly pleasant, with amorphously liberal entrance requirements. Lockwood, conceiving of Gimmerton and its environs as "a perfect misanthropist's heaven," speaks more truly than he means, and flees as soon after his enlightenment as he can. Heathcliff—who redefines Catherine's heaven as her hell—holds his heaven to be simply union with Catherine, and his hell, separation from her. Ideally, the setting for their union would be the moor, on "a dark evening threatening thunder." Even Joseph has his "sort of elysium," consisting of "a roaring fire"—Joseph could not stand to be too far from the flames of hell—"a quart of ale on the table near him, bristling with large pieces of toasted oat cake, and his black, short pipe in his mouth." And, I may add, a suffering sinner—here, Linton—loudly complaining in the next room. The several heavens of *Wuthering Heights* are merely the characters' antagonistic points of view raised to a higher power and projected into eternity.

Finally, through the notion of degradation, attention is called to inconclusive conceptual warfare not only among various characters but, more important, within Catherine Earnshaw and Heathcliff themselves. "Lowness" depends on one's scale of reference, of course. Edgar refers to Heathcliff's "baseness," calling him a "low ruffian," and Heathcliff, in retort, calls Edgar a "lamb," "not worth knocking down." Edgar's scale of values here depends on a social hierarchy, birth and refinement determining worth; Heathcliff's depends on the hierarchy of the wilds, might determining worth. Both standards are used by various characters: occasionally someone other than Heathcliff or Catherine Earnshaw will apply the latter standard (the second Catherine commands Linton, "Rise, and don't degrade yourself into an abject reptile"); but everyone, including even Catherine Earnshaw and Heathcliff, adopts the former standard. In fact much of Catherine's and Heathcliff's confusion and distress comes about because they do adopt it, more or less unawares and against their natures.

Catherine assumes the Lintons' scale of values in rejecting the possibility of marrying Heathcliff: "If the wicked man in there had not brought Heathcliff so low, I shouldn't have thought of [marrying Edgar]. It would degrade me to marry Heathcliff now." "If I marry Linton, I can aid Heathcliff to rise." For her, the received upper-class/lower-class scale of values is extended to include heaven/hell: "I've no more business to marry Edgar Linton than I have to be in heaven." Goodness is equated with social graces; salvation, with a genteel existence—with marriage to Edgar. These too simple terms are the only ones that she knows. She senses their inadequacy, but, in her innocence, she is unable to correct them or to supply alternative terms of value that do justice to Heathcliff and her feelings for him. She does suggest a reversal of values in likening her love for the elevated Edgar to transitory "foliage," and her attachment to the "low" Heathcliff to "the eternal rocks beneath." But she is unable to translate imagery into principles, and, therefore, in part out of her strong desire to do right, she marries Edgar.

Unlike Catherine, Heathcliff never questions the worth of his deepest attachment, finding her always "so immeasurably superior" to the Lintons. But like her, he never articulates or really understands the code of strength, vitality, and deep feeling basic to his nature. Nor is he true to it, being drawn, like her, to the code of the Lintons. "Nelly, make me decent, I'm going to be good." In an ill-conceived and futile effort to please Catherine, he adopts the values that she has adopted. When he overhears her confession that it would degrade her to marry him, he runs away, determined to out-Linton Edgar, and returns, having "raise[d] his mind from the savage ignorance into which it was sunk." His face now "looked intelligent, and retained no marks of former degradation." The terms are Nelly's, but Heathcliff himself would accept them. Nevertheless, Catherine, despite her excitement at his reappearance, never mentions his transformation, and she has already married Edgar. Edgar, seeing him still as "the plough-boy," is still an obstacle. Heathcliff's new, genteel self has changed nothing. He therefore adopts less civilized, more brutal modes of approaching Catherine. But he continues to wear his cloak of gentility loosely, employing it in the service of revenge upon Hindley and Edgar, the perpetrator and beneficiary of his original "degradation." As Arnold Kettle has observed, Heathcliff manages "to turn on them [stripped of their romantic veils] their own standards, to beat them at their own game. The weapons he uses against the Earnshaws and Lintons are their own weapons of money and arranged marriages."

It is important to realize, however, that Heathcliff adopts their standards, not out of a keen sense of irony or poetic justice, but simply because he does not discern any others. Heathcliff's goals are still the attainment of high station—wealth and property—with the consequent "degradation" of his enemies. As we have seen, he tries to relive his life in the following generation, with his son marrying the Catherine, and Hindley's son becoming the "low" Heathcliff. His continued but confused reliance on the standards of gentility is revealed in his remarking to Nelly of Hareton, "I've got him faster than his . . . father secured me, and lower; for he takes a pride in his brutishness. I've taught him to scorn everything extra-animal as silly and weak. Don't you think Hindley would be proud of his son . . . almost as proud as I am of mine. But there's this difference; one is gold put to the use of paving stones, and the other is tin polished to ape a service of silver. *Mine* has nothing valuable about it." Hareton is "lower" only according to the code of the Lintons, which Heathcliff only superficially embraces. All else in the passage tells the other way. "Pride" in brutishness and "scorn" for everything extra-animal imply another scale of values: the hierarchy of the wilds, which is basic to Heathcliff's nature, but which he does not fully appreciate or follow. Like Catherine, Heathcliff reveals his fundamental feelings in his images—gold, tin—but then proceeds, nevertheless, to act according to his adopted, articulated standards. Only when this second, vicarious attempt to top the ladder of gentility fails does he revert to his Catherine and the animal code that they both have betrayed. And even then he can neither explain his aberrant behavior nor articulate his fundamental values. In a larger sense than Lockwood, Heathcliff, for all his strength, stumbles ineptly through a world of pitfalls and concealed landmarks.

Whether it take place among characters or within a single character, an interaction of concepts results in inconclusive acrimony or inept groping. Conceptual conflict is not presented as a means to vision, but rather as a device to expose shortsightedness and indicate its consequences.

With all the characters myopic, and all their exchanges unilluminating, the reader looks elsewhere for authorial guidance. If the novelist does not present her own outlook directly, through her characters or their exchanges, the reader looks behind them for tokens of her controlling conception. He looks for signs of the author's working upon the reader's attitudes and point of view—for signs of the author's bringing the reader's views into line with her own.

Emily Brontë does not explicitly condemn or approve of her characters, nor does she imply judgment through the introduction of a machinery of rewards and punishments responsive to a moral order. But the reader is clearly expected to render verdicts; indeed he is induced to do so. Emily Brontë calls attention to judging by having Nelly Dean remark to Lockwood, "you'll judge as well as I can, all these things; at least you'll think you will, and that's the same." The remark—almost taunting, directed really at the reader by the author herself—causes us to question our own judgments of what she has presented, as well as those of Nelly and Lockwood. Inept moral judgments are a pervasive motif of this "amoral" book, and the reader is challenged or teased to do better. The vaguely annoying sensation of having trouble making up one's mind is a large part of the experience of reading *Wuthering Heights*.

As we have seen, the codes of judgment of all the characters cancel each other: Joseph's stern evangelicalism, Nelly's pragmatic preservation of the norm, Edgar's code of gentility, Heathcliff's law of the jungle, Linton's pure egocentrism. One character sees healthful tranquillity endangered by destructive violence; another sees fulfilling, expressive passion endangered by stifling repression. The shut windows protect, but they also incarcerate; open, they free, but they also destroy. The coward is offset by the bully; the boor by the snob; obstinacy by spinelessness; extremism by moderation at all costs. After closing the book, the reader can rest with the apprehension of an ethical deadlock, or he can choose sides according to the bias of his own nature. But in the actual process of reading the book, he is drawn beyond mere apprehension of the confused, indecisive conflicts to the point of actual participation in them. *Wuthering Heights* consistently encourages the reader to take sides, and then, by introducing behavior or descriptions against the grain of his expectations, to change sides.

Sometimes the betrayed judgments are simple matters of surprising characterization. Heathcliff, of all people, "retained a great deal of the reserve for which his boyhood was remarkable, and that served to repress all startling demonstrations of feeling." "Always [retire] at nine in winter, and always rise at four" is spoken by Heathcliff, not Nelly. Heathcliff, not Edgar, refers to his "temperate mode of living, and unperilous occupations." Heathcliff, not Edgar, "had an aversion to yielding so completely to his feelings." "Hush! Hush this moment!" are the words of Catherine Earnshaw, not Nelly. And " 'If you don't let me in, I'll kill you! If you don't let me in, I'll kill you!' he rather shrieked than said. 'Devil! devil! I'll kill you, I'll kill you!' " is not Heathcliff but the languid Linton. Besides demonstrating that "we've allas summut uh orther side in us," Emily Brontë is also disrupting the reader's too easy views of the characters and of the novel, if not of the act of conceptualization itself.

Edgar's striking Heathcliff a disabling blow is another such example. In fact Edgar's nature is tantalizingly plastic. At times he seems without strong feelings. (According to Nelly, "he wanted spirit in general.") At other times he seems to possess strong feelings, but to repress them strictly, as in his resorting to his library in the aftermath of his quarrel with his wife. Catherine here calls him "apathetic," but she is wrong, in part because she is misled by Nelly's slanted account of his behavior. At still other times he expresses strong feeling all too easily: He undergoes an "access of emotion," which causes him to tremble before Heathcliff; and he breaks into tears when his wife speaks well of his rival. The latter characterizations certainly complicate Lord David Cecil's division of the characters into "storms" and "calms"; for Edgar and other "calms" have their stormy moments as well as Heathcliff. The difference between them is rather one of mode of expression—and repression—or perhaps one of *basic* nature, than of clear polarity.

Lockwood's violence toward Jabes Branderham is another example of Emily Brontë's making it difficult for the reader to rely on his initial impressions of a character. Lockwood has just been presented as a helpless, rather effete foil to the animal, truly misanthropic Heathcliff, yet his behavior in the dream is exactly that of the young Heathcliff and Catherine, who also protest explosively, after having squirmed through a three-hour sermon by Joseph. In his second dream, Lockwood is savagely cruel, like Heathcliff, in gashing the child's wrist across the broken pane; but then he reverts to Edgar Linton's methods, as he piles up a buffer of books to prevent the entrance of the wild and stormy Catherine. Lockwood is alternately happy warrior and repressive milksop. The alternation tends to dissipate any symbolic charge that the reader might see in him.

Sometimes the unsettling of the reader's expectations is a more profound matter, challenging not only his simple perceptions of character and event, but his evaluations as well. When Nelly begins her account of Heathcliff, we are very sympathetic toward him, because of such details as the other children's rejecting and plaguing him, his stoicism in punishment, and his long suffering in sickness. Nelly's coming over to take his side only reinforces our first, favorable impression. But then Nelly recounts the instance of Heathcliff's forcing Hindley to trade horses with him. The episode supports points that she has already made—e.g., Hindley's abuse of Heathcliff, and Heathcliff's coolness under punishment—but Nelly has not prepared us for a provoking insolence on the part of Heathcliff ("You must exchange horses with me; I don't like mine, and if you won't I shall tell your father"), in addition to a scheming and an outrageous greed (Heathcliff had taken the handsomest colt to begin with). Hindley is clearly being wronged, and our sympathies undergo a momentary reversal. But Nelly closes by reemphasizing Heathcliff's ability to withstand pain and praising his indifference to pursuing his advantage over Hindley—his refusing to carry his bruises before Mr. Earnshaw. Thus our original sympathies are largely restored, but shaken.

Elsewhere we are far from being on Heathcliff's side when he takes to twisting the arms, characters, and destinies of helpless women and children. His calling his behavior "moral teething" or our recognizing that he is acting as he does because of his powerful, thwarted feelings for Catherine does not really satisfy our sense of justice. G. D. Klingopulos rightly refers to these scenes as "painful," in which "deliberate violence is done to our ideas of elementary kindness and fairness, in which brute force asserts itself in the place of love and kindness." The pain comes not so much from the sight of wounds as from outrageous wrongs unrighted. At the time we do not begin to justify or sympathize with Heathcliff. Yet elsewhere, when he says, for example, "as to repenting of my injustices, I've done no injustice, and I repent of nothing," we are so caught up with his own declarations of suffering—his being killed, over eighteen years, "not by inches, but by fractions of hair breadths"—that we dismiss his frightful cruelty to others as incidental and quite justified under the circumstances. In short, we are being inconsistent—we are guilty of employing the "nowt"-device. Our allegiances are being toyed with, as *Wuthering Heights* plays a shell game with our sympathies.

Nor does the ending of the novel relieve the reader's quandary. The ending is ambiguous (as Klingopulos has observed), with respect to both meaning and event. Obviously Emily Brontë concludes in a severely geometric way: completing the perfect circle from Hareton Earnshaw, 1500, to Hareton Earnshaw, 1802; drawing the marriage triangle of Linton, Cathy, and Hareton; and working out the absolute symmetry of the pedigree, which C. P. Sanger has noted. Emily Brontë may be implying something about order emerging from apparent chaos. But her order is not that of comprehensive reconciliation or resolution. The harmony with which she concludes does not come about through a resolution of the warring elements. These have rather been set aside, or projected beyond the grave, and new elements substituted.

A child raised by Edgar can join in happy marriage with a child raised by Heathcliff, the foster mother of both children being the genius of compatibility, Nelly. But the marriage between Cathy and Hareton says little about any symbolic reconciliation between Edgar and Heathcliff, or any surrogate, compensatory marriage between Heathcliff and the first Catherine. For Hareton is not really another Heathcliff, and Cathy Linton is neither her father nor her mother. Hareton is slovenly and uncouth, but he does not possess Heathcliff's savagery and wild passion. His puppy-hanging notwithstanding, he does not have the killer instinct. Cathy Linton is much more perambulatory than her father, more exploratory and accepting, more vital. She does not repress and deny to the extent that he does. And although, like her mother, she judges unwisely, marrying the wrong, too effete man first, her essential nature and her grounds for ultimate compatibility fall well within the pale of civilization and sociability, as her mother's do not. Cathy and Hareton are reminiscent of the previous generation, but they are not really representative of them. The most that can be said is tautological: They symbolize the reconciliation of those elements in Heathcliff, Edgar, and Catherine Earnshaw that admit of reconciliation. They are moderates, adventurous only in the direction of the normal, the middle way. "Con-*trary*" rings false on their lips.

It is equally hard to salvage any new, clear meaning from the other closing event, the death of Heathcliff. The disposition of the three graves retells the story of the three lives: Catherine, closer to Heathcliff, but caught between contraries nevertheless. In twisting Heathcliff's and Edgar's locks together and placing them in Catherine's locket, Nelly Dean had expressed the sugared hope that everyone will get along with everyone else, and die, at least, happily ever after. Her act, like the marriage of Cathy Linton and Hareton, teases the reader into seeing the three as somehow reconciled at last. But Nelly's general obtuseness, as well as the ambiguous symbolism of her gesture—Heathcliff and Edgar could be locked in battle as well as friendship—render her gesture enigmatical, if not meaningless.

Of course Heathcliff sees triumph over Edgar and union with Catherine in his death. But there is no good reason for removing his hopeful remarks from the corrosive context of the novel—no reason for granting his expectations a special credence. He professes "a strong faith in ghosts; I have a conviction that they can, and do exist, among us!" but the strength of his belief in them is no warrant for their existence. His remarks finally show great feeling rather than good vision. And others believe otherwise; as we have seen, his notion of heaven is only one among many, and he has not distinguished himself elsewhere for perspicacity. We are given no basis for deciding whether his view of the afterlife is any more valid than, for example, Edgar's vision of a more restful sleep at Catherine's side. At the close we find two versions of Heathcliff after death, one from a suggestible and superstitious shepherd boy, who believes that he has seen Heathcliff and Catherine together on the moor; the other, from Nelly and Lockwood, who reinforce each other's cozy sense of the familiar by proclaiming the boy's story "nonsense" and by wondering "how any one could ever imagine unquiet slumbers for the sleepers in that quiet earth." Thus *Wuthering Heights* concludes in characteristic fashion, with two accounts, both suspect, blunting each other, and with Emily Brontë supplying the puzzled reader with no privileged vantage point to relieve his uncertainty.

Instead of gradually aligning the reader's outlook with some controlling point of view of her own, Emily Brontë systematically brings it into line with the various limited perspectives of her characters. We are granted no visions, only variations upon the experience of shortsightedness. Although it is not unusual for a reader, in the course of a novel, to be led to change his mind about a character or event, he is accustomed to make his revisions upward—to find his perceptions coming closer to the full truth as it is presented by the author. *Wuthering Heights* is remarkable in that the tokens of authorial guidance serve throughout to keep the reader down, to make him grope and stumble.

Because Emily Brontë frustrates any alliance with her reader, it is finally impossible to know her mind with respect to *Wuthering Heights*. I can only speculate upon her intentions concerning the motif of limited vision. First, I do believe the effects I have set forth to be the products of deliberation. Although one resists ascribing to anyone's first novel the subtle laminations of a Henry James, the remark, "you'll judge as well as I can, all these things; at least you'll think you will, and that's the same," shows Emily Brontë to be aware enough of Lockwood's—and the reader's—perplexities to mock them for them. Moreover, the sheer number of details that treat limited vision (and I have omitted many) suggests conscious intention—suggests a program. The details I adduce, then, ought not to be dismissed as accidental, but are to be reckoned with.

Second, I cannot accept the notion that Emily Brontë is perplexing her characters out of mere whimsy, or that she is playing a hoax on her reader. Although I have taken pains to point out ambiguous aspects of the novel, I would say that everything about it points clearly to the seriousness of the author's intentions.

Third, I reject with some hesitation the possibility that Emily Brontë baffles the reader in order to effect the best hearing for a preternatural truth. It is certainly understandable that, with such an end in mind, an author would distance the reader from her wonders, would wrap them in a haze and provide such alternative, commonsense explanations as would keep him from feeling trapped, thus making him more generous or adventurous in his suppositions. Although my presentation of *Wuthering Heights* is largely compatible with this interpretation, I finally reject it because I feel that Emily Brontë renders her reader less rather than more ready to speculate. Instead of providing him a back door, so to speak, she presents him with a veritable labyrinth of alternatives. And rather than leaving him alone in their midst to choose and be tempted, she shuttles him about among them, checking in turn his every incipient formulation and sympathy. The reader has sporadically been made to see too much truth in the way that Nelly, Lockwood, Edgar, Cathy Linton, or even Joseph sees things to be able to accept wholly the dying Heathcliff's expectations. And he has finally seen too much blindness and confusion in all, including himself, to trust the grand views of anyone.

My best guess is that Emily Brontë does not pretend to an overarching vision, and that that is her point. The stumbling shortsightedness that she presents in her characters and induces in her reader is in fact her own experience of the world and the burden of her message. She does not expect the reader to embrace any world view, not even the attractively Romantic, elemental, animistic one implicit in the relationship between Heathcliff and Catherine. She expects the reader rather to experience with them the sense of it as looming intangibly and uncertainly just beyond their ken, even as it is naggingly gainsaid, crossed by ineradicably foreground considerations. In a word, she presents wuthering as basic to almost all human experience.

This reading emphasizes Heathcliff's and Catherine's similarity to all other characters. The force and length of Heathcliff's and Catherine's struggles, and their divided selves, which reflect the novel's outer divisions, mark them as superior to the others, but they are not essentially different nor is their predicament unique. What we admire most about them is not any special vision with which they have been blessed or any special "mystical vocation" that they have been granted, but rather their greater suffering in the grip of the human condition, and, ineffectual though it may be, their greater resistance to it.

Emily Brontë is finally depicting a Victorian rather than a Romantic state of mind, one akin to Arnold's

> Hither and thither spins
> The wind-borne mirroring soul,
> A thousand glimpses wins,
> And never sees a whole
> (*Empedocles on Etna*, ll. 6–9)

One akin also to George Eliot's sense of the futility of human ordering implicit in her celebrated image of a pier-glass, "multitudinously scratched in all directions," which yet presents a unique pattern of concentric circles of scratches to each candle held up to it (*Middlemarch,* chap. 27). Like many of her fellow Victorians, Emily Brontë would seem to have been impressed by multiplicity of outlook and the relativity inherent in any point of view. That she would choose to employ the Romantic vision as her primary example of a concept felt to be receding beyond human viability places her almost too neatly as a transitional figure between the literary periods.

One thing at least is clear: Whatever her intentions, Emily Brontë did not merely throw her being vicariously into the lives of Heathcliff and Catherine. That she did read herself into their fictive adventures goes without saying. But an equally strong impulse was her drawing back in acid judgment: upon her Romantic characters, as well as the more conventional characters who cross their existence. By implicating the reader as well, she dramatized the truth and range of her strictures. Her Romantic impulse was severely checked, if not actually destroyed, by the critical, judicial impulse. It has been said of her that she "never casts a sidelong glance; she is innocent of irony." Clearly the remark is incorrect, insofar as irony is used in the sense given currency by T. S. Eliot, namely, a strong awareness of alternative possibilities and points of view. A sidelong glance questions every view in *Wuthering Heights*. She has also been called a visionary. It is true that she often gives her reader a sense of vital forces operating just beyond the horizons of humanity. But, far from pretending to see beyond the sight of other men, she stresses the faults and limited scope of all human sight. Her final vision—epistemological, fragmented, negative—is a very earthly one, very close to home.

A Modern Way with the Classic

Frank Kermode

Horace provided a rule of thumb, sensible so far as it goes, when he said: *est vetus atque probus, centum qui perfecit annos;* he did not know the word "classic" in the literary sense, but Pope was right to put it into his imitation of Horace's line:

> Who lasts a century can have no flaw,
> I hold that Wit a Classic, good in law.

What they leave out is an account of the temporal agencies of survival, the most important of which is a more or less continuous chorus of voices asserting the value of the classic; and of course they say nothing about the difficulties that arise in consequence of periodic changes in language, generic expectation, ideology, and so forth. The imperialist view of the classic accommodates all these. . . . It does so by modifications of the basic model (renovations, translations, and the like) and by other means we can broadly call allegorical. But ultimately it rests on the notion of a moment privileged, timeless yet capable of contemporaneity with all others, a classic in which all lesser classics participate. If we were to think of theirs as a scientific theory we should reject it either as we reject Ptolemaic astronomy (because discrepancies between the model and observational data require too many new rules—epicycles, *translationes*—for the model itself to remain credible; a new model is required) or more simply because it is not, as Popper would say, testable. It is easy to see that such criteria have relevance. And yet such

From *The Classic: Literary Images of Permanence and Change.* © 1975 by Frank Kermode. Viking Press, 1975.

models change, by other and perhaps obscurer laws. We are less able to rest easy with the imperial model in its purity.

A new model would require us in the first place to abandon the notion of the absolute classic and consider, more simply, the Horatian case, the text which continues to be read several generations after it was written. A classic, then, is a book that is read a long time after it was written; one might want to qualify this by adding "without institutional constraint," "by the competent," and perhaps other rules. Once we made this new start we can see some of the problems in quite a different light. *Translationes* become transitions from a past to a present system of beliefs, language, generic expectations; renovations become very specific attempts to establish the relevance of a document which has had a good chance of losing it. The *querelle* persists, but with major changes in the historiographical assumptions of the two sides.

These are some of the topics I have to consider in this [essay]. There are others, all related to the ones I have mentioned; the most important is the extreme variety of response characteristic of the modern reading of the classic. But I daresay it is best to approach these questions by way of a single familiar text; and I have chosen *Wuthering Heights* for what I take to be good reasons. It meets the requirement that it is read in a generation far separated from the one it was presented to; and it has other less obvious advantages. It happens that I had not read the novel for many years; furthermore, although I could not be unaware that it had suffered a good deal of interpretation, and had been the centre of quarrels, I had also omitted to read any of this secondary material. These chances put me in a position unfamiliar to the teacher of literature; I could consider my own response to a classic more or less untrammelled by too frequent reading, and by knowledge of what it had proved possible, or become customary, to say about it. This strikes me as a happy situation, though some may call it shameful. Anyway, it is the best way I can think of to arrive at some general conclusions about the classic, though I daresay those conclusions will sound more like a programme for research than a true ending to this briefer exercise.

I begin, then, with a partial reading of *Wuthering Heights* which represents a straightforward encounter between a competent modern reader (the notion of competence is, I think, essential however much you may think this demonstration falls short of it) and a classic text. However, in assuming this role, I could not avoid noticing some remarks that are not in the novel at all, but in Charlotte Brontë's Biographical Notice of her sisters, in which she singles out a contemporary critic as the only one who got her sister's book right. "Too often," she says, "do reviewers remind us of the mob of Astrologers, Chaldeans and Soothsayers gathered before the 'writing on the wall,' and unable to read the characters or make known the interpretation." One, however, has accurately read "the Mene, Mene, Tekel, Upharsin of an original mind" and "can say with confidence, 'This is the interpretation thereof.' " This latterday Daniel was Signey Dobell, but a modern reader who looks him up in the hope of coming upon what would after all be a very valuable piece of information is likely to be disappointed. Very few would dream of doing so; most would mistrust the critic for whom such claims were made, or the book which lent itself to them. Few would believe that such an interpretation exists, however frequently the critics produce new "keys." For we don't think of the novel as a code, or a nut, that can be broken; which contains or refers to a meaning all will agree upon if it can once be presented *en clair*. We need little persuasion to believe that a good novel is not a message at all. We assume in principle the rightness of the plurality of interpretations to which I now, in ignorance of all the others, but reasonably confident that I won't repeat them, now contribute.

When Lockwood first visits Wuthering Heights he notices, among otherwise irrelevant decorations carved above the door, the date *1500* and the name *Hareton Earnshaw*. It is quite clear that everybody read and reads this as a sort of promise of something else to come. It is part of what is nowadays called a "hermeneutic code"; something that promises, and perhaps after some delay provides, explanation. There is, of course, likely to be some measure of peripeteia or trick; you would be surprised if the explanation were not, in some way, surprising, or at any rate, at this stage unpredictable. And so it proves. The expectations aroused by these inscriptions are strictly *generic;* you must know things of this kind before you can entertain expectations of the sort I mention. Genre in this sense is what Leonard Meyer (writing of music) calls "an internalized probability system." Such a system could, but perhaps shouldn't, be thought of as constituting some sort of contract between reader and writer. Either way, the inscriptions can be seen as something other than simple elements in a series of one damned thing after another, or even of events relative to a story as such. They reduce the range of probabilities, reduce randomness, and are expected to recur. There will be "feedback." This may not extinguish all the informational possibilities in the original stimulus, which may be, and in this case is, obscurer than we thought, "higher," as the information theorists say, "in entropy." The narrative is more than merely a lengthy delay, after which a true descendant of Hareton Earnshaw reoccupies the ancestral house; though there is a little delay before we hear about him, and can make a guess if we want.

When Hareton is first discussed, Nelly Dean rather oddly describes him as "the late Mrs. Linton's nephew." Why not "the late Mr. Earnshaw's son"? It is only in the previous sentence that we have first heard the name Linton, when the family of that name is mentioned as having previously occupied Thrushcross Grange. Perhaps we are to wonder how Mrs. Linton came to have a nephew named Earnshaw. At any rate, Nelly's obliquity thus serves to associate Hareton, in a hazy way, with the house on which his name is *not* carved, and with a family no longer in evidence. Only later do we discover that he is in the direct Earnshaw line, in fact, as Nelly says, "the last of them." So begins the provision of information which both fulfils and qualifies the early "hermeneutic" promise; because, of course, Hareton, his inheritance restored, goes to live at the Grange. The two principal characters remaining at the end are Mr. and Mrs. Hareton Earnshaw. The other names, which have intruded on Earnshaw—Linton and Heathcliff—are extinct. In between there have been significant recursions to the original inscription—in chapter 20 Hareton cannot read it; in 24 he can read the name but not the date.

We could say, I suppose, that this so far tells us nothing about *Wuthering Heights* that couldn't, with appropriate changes, be said of most novels. All of them contain the equivalent of such inscriptions; indeed all writing is a sort of inscription, cut memorably into the uncaused flux of event; and inscriptions of the kind I am talking about are interesting secondary clues about the nature of the writing in which they occur. They draw attention to the literariness of what we are reading, indicate that the story is a story, perhaps with beneficial effects on our normal powers of perception; above all they distinguish a *literary* system which has no constant relation to readers with interests and expectations altered by long passages of time. Or, to put it another way, Emily Brontë's contemporaries operated different probability systems from ours, and might well ignore whatever in a text did not comply with their generic expectations, dismissing the rest somehow—by skipping, by accusations of bad craftsmanship, inexperience, or the like. In short, their internalized probability systems survive them in altered and less stringent forms; we can read more of the text than they could, and of course read it differently. In fact, the only works we value enough to call classic are those which, and they demonstrate by surviving, are complex and indeterminate enough to allow us our necessary pluralities. That "Mene, Mene, Tekel, Upharsin" has now many interpretations. It is in the nature of works of art to be open, in so far as they are "good"; though it is in the nature of authors, and of readers, to close them.

The openness of *Wuthering Heights* might be somewhat more exten-
sively illustrated by an inquiry into the passage describing Lockwood's bad
night at the house, when, on his second visit, he was cut off from Thrushcross Grange by a storm. He is given an odd sort of bed in a bedroom-
within-a-bedroom; Catherine Earnshaw slept in it and later Heathcliff
would die in it. Both the bed and the lattice are subjects of very elaborate
"play"; but I want rather to consider the inscriptions Lockwood examines
before retiring. There is writing on the wall, or on the ledge by his bed: it
"was nothing but a name repeated in all kinds of characters, large and
small—*Catherine Earnshaw,* here and there varied to *Catherine Heathcliff,* and
then again to *Catherine Linton.*" When he closes his eyes Lockwood is
assailed by white letters "which started from the dark, as vivid as spectres—
the air swarmed with Catherines." He has no idea whatever to whom these
names belong, yet the expression "nothing but a name" seems to suggest
that they all belong to one person. Waking from a doze he finds the name
Catherine Earnshaw inscribed in a book his candle has scorched.

It is true that Lockwood has earlier met a Mrs. Heathcliff, and got into
a tangle about who she was, taking first Heathcliff and then Hareton Earnshaw for her husband, as indeed, we discover she, in a different sense, had
also done or was to do. For she had a merely apparent kinship relation with
Heathcliff—bearing his name as the wife of his impotent son and having
to tolerate his ironic claim to fatherhood—as a prelude to the restoration
of her true name, Earnshaw; it is her mother's story reversed. But Lockwood was not told her first name. Soon he is to encounter a ghost called
Catherine Linton; but if the scribbled names signify one person he and we
are obviously going to have to wait to find who it is. Soon we learn
that Mrs. Heathcliff is Heathcliff's daughter-in-law, *née* Catherine Linton,
and obviously not the ghost. Later it becomes evident that the scratcher
must have been Catherine Earnshaw, later Linton, a girl long dead who
might well have been Catherine Heathcliff, but wasn't.

When you have processed all the information you have been waiting
for you see the point of the order of the scribbled names, as Lockwood
gives them: *Catherine Earnshaw, Catherine Heathcliff, Catherine Linton.* Read
from left to right they recapitulate Catherine Earnshaw's story; read from
right to left, the story of her daughter, Catherine Linton. The names Catherine and Earnshaw begin and end the narrative. Of course some of the
events needed to complete this pattern had not occurred when Lockwood
slept in the little bedroom; indeed the marriage of Hareton and Catherine
is still in the future when the novel ends. Still, this is an account of the
movement of the book: away from Earnshaw and back, like the movement
of the house itself. And all the movement must be *through* Heathcliff.

Charlotte Brontë remarks, from her own experience, that the writer says more than he knows, and was emphatic that this was so with Emily. "Having formed these beings, she did not know what she had done." Of course this strikes us as no more than common sense; though Charlotte chooses to attribute it to Emily's ignorance of the world. A narrative is not a transcription of something preexistent. And this is precisely the situation represented by Lockwood's play with the names he does not understand, his constituting, out of many scribbles, a rebus for the plot of the novel he's in. The situation indicates the kind of work we must do when a narrative opens itself to us, and contains information in excess of what generic probability requires.

Consider the names again; of course they reflect the isolation of the society under consideration, but still it is remarkable that in a story whose principal characters all marry there are effectively only three surnames, all of which each Catherine assumes. Furthermore, the Earnshaw family makes do with only three Christian names, Catherine, Hindley, Hareton. Heathcliff is a family name also, but parsimoniously, serving as both Christian name and surname; always lacking one or the other, he wears his name as an indication of his difference, and this persists after death since his tombstone is inscribed with the one word *Heathcliff*. Like Frances, briefly the wife of Hindley, he is simply a sort of interruption in the Earnshaw system.

Heathcliff is then as it were between names, as between families (he is the door through which Earnshaw passes into Linton, and out again to Earnshaw). He is often introduced, as if characteristically, standing outside, or entering, or leaving, a door. He is in and out of the Earnshaw family simultaneously; servant and child of the family (like Hareton, whom he puts in the same position, he helps to indicate the archaic nature of the house's society, the lack of sharp social division, which is not characteristic of the Grange). His origins are equally betwixt and between: the gutter or the royal origin imagined for him by Nelly; prince or pauper, American or Lascar, child of God or devil. This betweenness persists, I think: Heathcliff, for instance, fluctuates between poverty and riches; also between virility and impotence. To Catherine he is between brother and lover; he slept with her as a child, and again in death, but not between latency and extinction. He has much force, yet fathers an exceptionally puny child. Domestic yet savage like the dogs, bleak yet full of fire like the house, he bestrides the great opposites: love and death (the necrophiliac confession), culture and nature ("half-civilized ferocity") in a posture that certainly cannot be explained by any generic formula ("Byronic" or "Gothic").

He stands also between a past and a future; when his force expires the old Earnshaw family moves into the future associated with the civilized Grange, where the insane authoritarianism of the Heights is a thing of the past, where there are cultivated distinctions between gentle and simple—a new world in the more civil south. It was the Grange that first separated Heathcliff from Catherine, so that Earnshaws might eventually live there. Of the children—Hareton, Cathy, and Linton—none physically resembles Heathcliff; the first two have Catherine's eyes (chap. 23) and the other is, as his first name implies, a Linton. Cathy's two cousin-marriages, constituting an endogamous route to the civilized exogamy of the south—are the consequence of Heathcliff's standing between Earnshaw and Linton, north and south; earlier he had involuntarily saved the life of the baby Hareton. His ghost and Catherine's, at the end, are of interest only to the superstitious, the indigenous now to be dispossessed by a more rational culture.

If we look, once more, at Lockwood's inscriptions, we may read them thus:

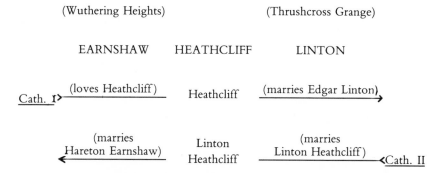

(Wuthering Heights)　　　　　　(Thrushcross Grange)

EARNSHAW　　HEATHCLIFF　　LINTON

Cath. I▷ —(loves Heathcliff)—　Heathcliff　—(marries Edgar Linton)→

—(marries Hareton Earnshaw)←　Linton Heathcliff　—(marries Linton Heathcliff)◁ Cath. II

N.B. Heathcliff stands between Earnshaw and Linton as having Earnshaw origins but marrying Isabella Linton. He could also be represented as moving from left to right to left—into the Linton column, and then back to the Earnshaw when he usurps the hereditary position of Hareton. Hareton himself might be represented as having first been forced out of the Earnshaw column into the intermediate position when Heathcliff reduces him to a position resembling the one he himself started from, a savage and inferior member of the family. But he returns to the Earnshaw column with Cath. II. Finally they move together (without passing through the intermediate position, which has been abolished) from left to right, from Wuthering Heights to Thrushcross Grange.

Earnshaws persist, but they must eventually do so within the Linton culture. Catherine burns up in her transit from left to right. The quasi-Earnshaw union of Heathcliff and Isabella leaves the younger Cathy an easier passage; she has only to get through Linton Heathcliff, who is replaced by Hareton Earnshaw, Hareton has suffered part of Heathcliff's fate, moved, as it were, from Earnshaw to Heathcliff, and replaced him as son-servant, as gratuitously cruel; but he is the last of the Earnshaws, and Cathy can both restore to him the house on which his name is carved, and take him on the now smooth path to Thrushcross Grange.

Novels, even this one, were read in houses more like the Grange than the Heights, as the emphasis on the ferocious piety of the Earnshaw library suggests. The order of the novel is a civilized order; it presupposes a reader in the midst of an educated family and habituated to novel reading; a reader, moreover, who believes in the possibility of effective ethical choices. And because this is the case, the author can allow herself to meet his proper expectations without imposing on the text or on him absolute generic control. She need not, that is, know all that she is saying. She can, in all manner of ways, invite the reader to collaborate, leave to him the supply of meaning where the text is indeterminate or discontinuous, where explanations are required to fill narrative lacunae.

Instances of this are provided by some of the dreams in the book. Lockwood's brief dream of the spectral letters is followed by another about an interminable sermon, which develops from hints about Joseph in Catherine's Bible. The purport of this dream is obscure. The preacher Jabes Branderham takes a hint from his text and expands the seven deadly sins into seventy times seven plus one. It is when he reaches the last section that Lockwood's patience runs out, and he protests, with his own allusion to the Bible: "He shall return no more to his house, neither shall his place know him any more." Dreams in stories are usually given a measure of oneiric ambiguity, but stay fairly close to the narrative line, or if not, convey information otherwise useful; but this one does not appear to do so, except in so far as that text may bear obscurely and incorrectly on the question of where Hareton will end up. It is, however, given a naturalistic explanation: the rapping of the preacher on the pulpit is a dream version of the rapping of the fir tree on the window.

Lockwood once more falls asleep, but dreams again, and "if possible, still more disagreeably than before." Once more he hears the fir-bough, and rises to silence it; he breaks the window and finds himself clutching the cold hand of a child who calls herself Catherine Linton.

He speaks of this as a dream, indeed he ascribes to it "the intense horror of nightmare," and the blood that runs down into the bedclothes may be explained by his having cut his hand as he broke the glass; but he does not say so, attributing it to his own cruelty in rubbing the child's wrist on the pane; and Heathcliff immediately makes it obvious that of the two choices the text has so far allowed us the more acceptable is that Lockwood was not dreaming at all.

So we cannot dismiss this dream as "Gothic" ornament or commentary, or even as the kind of dream Lockwood has just had, in which the same fir-bough produced a comically extended dream-explanation of its presence. There remain all manner of puzzles: why is the visitant a child and, if a child, why Catherine *Linton?* The explanation, that this name got into Lockwood's dream from a scribble in the Bible is one even he finds hard to accept. He hovers between an explanation involving "ghosts and goblins," and the simpler one of nightmare; though he has no more doubt than Heathcliff that "it"—the child—was trying to enter. For good measure he is greeted, on going downstairs, by a cat, a brindled cat, with its echo of Shakespearian witchcraft.

It seems plain, then, that the dream is not simply a transformation of the narrative, a commentary on another level, but an integral part of it. The Branderham dream is, in a sense, a trick, suggesting a measure of rationality in the earlier dream which we might want to transfer to the later experience, as Lockwood partly does. When we see that there is a considerable conflict in the clues as to how we should read the second tapping and relate it to the first we grow aware of further contrasts between the two, for the first is a comic treatment of 491 specific and resistible sins for which Lockwood is about to be punished by exile from his home, and the second is a more horrible spectral invasion of the womb-like or tomb-like room in which he is housed. There are doubtless many other observations to be made; it is not a question of deciding which is the single right reading, but of dealing, as reader, with a series of indeterminacies which the text will not resolve.

Nelly Dean refuses to listen to Catherine's dream, one of those which went through and through her "like wine through water"; and of those dreams we hear nothing save this account of their power. "We're dismal enough without conjuring up ghosts and visions to perplex us," says Nelly—another speaking silence in the text, for it is implied that we are here denied relevant information. But she herself suffers a dream or vision. After Heathcliff's return she finds herself at the signpost: engraved in its sandstone—with all the permanence that Hareton's name has on the house— are "Wuthering Heights" to the north, "Gimmerton" to the east, and "Thrushcross Grange" to the south. Soft south, harsh north, and the rough civility of the market town (something like that of Nelly herself) in between. As before, these inscriptions provoke a dream apparition, a vision of Hindley as a child. Fearing that he has come to harm, she rushes to the Heights and again sees the spectral child, but it turns out to be Hareton, Hindley's son. His appearance betwixt and between the Heights and the Grange was proleptic; now he is back at the Heights, a stone in his hand, threatening his old nurse, rejecting the Grange. And as Hindley turned into Hareton, so Hareton turns into Heathcliff, for the figure that appears in the doorway is Heathcliff.

This is very like a real dream in its transformations and displacements. It has no simple narrative function whatever, and an abridgement might leave it out. But the confusion of generations, and the double usurpation of Hindley by his son and Heathcliff, all three of them variants of the incivility of the Heights, gives a new relation to the agents, and qualifies our sense of all narrative explanations offered in the text. For it is worth remarking that no naturalistic explanation of Nelly's experience is offered; in this it is unlike the treatment of the later vision, when the little boy sees the ghost of Heathcliff and "a woman," a passage which is a preparation for further ambiguities in the ending. Dreams, visions, ghosts—the whole pneumatology of the book is only indeterminately related to the "natural" narrative. And this serves to muddle routine "single" readings, to confound explanation and expectation, and to make necessary a full recognition of the intrinsic plurality of the text.

Would it be reasonable to say this: that the mingling of generic opposites—daylight and dream narratives—creates a need, which we must supply, for something that will mediate between them? If so, we can go on to argue that the text in our response to it is a provision of such mediators, between life and death, the barbaric and the civilized, family and sexual relations. The principal instrument of mediation may well be Heathcliff: neither inside nor out, neither wholly master nor wholly servant, the husband who is no husband, the brother who is no brother, the father who abuses his changeling child, the cousin without kin. And that the chain of narrators serve to mediate between the barbarism of the story and the civility of the reader—making the text itself an intermediate term between archaic and modern—must surely have been pointed out.

What we must not forget, however, is that it is in the completion of the text by the reader that these adjustments are made; and each reader will make them differently. Plurality is here not a prescription but a fact. There is so much that is blurred and tentative, incapable of decisive explanation; however we set about our reading, with a sociological or a pneumatological, a cultural or a narrative code uppermost in our minds, we must fall into division and discrepancy; the doors of communication are sometimes locked, sometimes open, and Heathcliff may be astride the threshold, opening, closing, breaking. And it is surely evident that the possibilities of interpretation increase as time goes on. The constraints of a period culture dissolve, generic presumptions which concealed gaps disappear, and we now see that the book, as James thought novels should, truly "glories in a gap," a hermeneutic gap in which the reader's imagination must operate, so that he speaks continuously in the text. For these reasons the rebus— *Catherine Earnshaw, Catherine Heathcliff, Catherine Linton*—has exemplary significance. It is a riddle that the text answers only silently; for example it will neither urge nor forbid you to remember that it resembles the riddle of the Sphinx—what manner of person exists in these three forms?—to which the single acceptable and probable answer involves incest and ruin.

I have not found it possible to speak of *Wuthering Heights* in this light without, from time to time, hinting—in a word here, or a trick of procedure there—at the new French criticism. I am glad to acknowledge this affinity, but it also seems important to dissent from the opinion that such "classic" texts as this—and the French will call them so, but with pejorative intent— are essentially naive, and become in a measure plural only by accident. The number of choices is simply too large; it is impossible that even two competent readers should agree on an authorized naive version. It is because texts are so naive that they can become classics. It is true, as I have said, that time opens them up; if readers were immortal the classic would be much closer to changelessness; their deaths do, in an important sense, liberate the texts. But to attribute the entire *potential* of plurality to that cause (or to the wisdom and cunning of later readers) is to fall into a mistake. The "Catherines" of Lockwood's inscriptions may not have been attended to, but there they were in the text, just as ambiguous and plural as they are now. What happens is that methods of repairing such indeterminacy change; and, as Wolfgang Iser's neat formula has it, "the repair of indeterminacy" is what gives rise "to the generation of meaning."

Having meditated thus on *Wuthering Heights* I passed to the second part of my enterprise and began to read what people have been saying about the book. I discovered without surprise that no two readers saw it exactly alike; some seemed foolish and some clever, but whether they were of the party that claims to elucidate Emily Brontë's intention, or libertarians whose purpose is to astonish us, all were different. This secondary material is voluminous, but any hesitation I might have had about selecting from it was ended when I came upon an essay which in its mature authority dwarfs all the others: Q. D. Leavis's "A Fresh Approach to *Wuthering Heights.*"

Long-meditated, rich in insights, this work has a sober force that nothing I say could, or is intended to, diminish. Mrs. Leavis remarks at the outset that merely to *assert* the classic status of such a book as *Wuthering Heights* is useless; that the task is not to be accomplished by ignoring "recalcitrant elements" or providing sophistical explanations of them. One has to show "the nature of its success"; and this, she at once proposes, means giving up some parts of the text. "Of course, in general one attempts to achieve a reading of a text which includes all its elements, but here I believe we must be satisfied with being able to account for some of them and concentrate on what remains." And she decides that Emily Brontë through inexperience, and trying to do too much, leaves in the final version vestiges of earlier creations, "unregenerate writing," which is discordant with the true "realistic novel" we should attend to.

She speaks of an earlier version deriving from *King Lear,* with Heathcliff as an Edmund figure, and attributes to this layer some contrived and unconvincing scenes of cruelty. Another layer is the fairy-story, Heathcliff as the prince transformed into a beast; another is the Romantic incest-story: Heathcliff as brother-lover; and nearer the surface, a sociological novel, of which she has no difficulty in providing, with material from the text, a skilful account. These vestiges explain some of the incongruities and inconsistencies of the novel—for example, the ambiguity of the Catherine-Heathcliff relationship—and have the effect of obscuring its "human centrality." To summarize a long and substantial argument, this real novel, which we come upon clearly when the rest is cut away, is founded on the contrast between the two Catherines, the one willing her own destruction, the other educated by experience and avoiding the same fate. Not only does this cast a new light on such characters as Joseph and Nelly Dean as representatives of a culture that, as well as severity, inculcates a kind of natural piety, but enables us to see Emily Brontë as "a true novelist . . . whose material was real life and whose concern was to promote a fine awareness of human relations and the problem of maturity." And we can't see this unless we reject a good deal of the text as belonging more to "self-indulgent story" than to the "responsible piece of work" Emily was eventually able to perform. Heathcliff we are to regard as "merely a convenience"; in a striking comparison with Dostoevsky's Stavrogin, Mrs. Leavis argues that he is "enigmatic . . . only by reason of his creator's indecision," and that to find reasons for thinking otherwise is "misguided critical industry." By the same token the famous passages about Catherine's love for Heathcliff are dismissed as rhetorical excesses, obstacles to the "real novel enacted so richly for us to grasp in all its complexity."

Now it seems very clear to me that the "real novel" Mrs. Leavis describes *is* there, in the text. It is also clear that she is aware of the danger in her own procedures, for she explains how easy it would be to account for *Wuthering Heights* as a sociological novel by discarding certain elements and concentrating on others, which, she says, would be "misconceiving the novel and slighting it." What she will not admit is that there is a sense in which all these versions are not only present but have a claim on our attention. She creates a hierarchy of elements, and does so by a peculiar archaeology of her own, for there is no *evidence* that the novel existed in the earlier forms which are supposed to have left vestiges in the only text we have, and there is no reason why the kind of speculation and conjecture on which her historical argument depends could not be practised with equal right by proponents of quite other theories. Nor can I explain why it seemed to her that the only way to establish hers as the central reading of the book was to explain the rest away; for there, after all, the others *are*. Digging and carbon-dating simply have no equivalents here; there is no way of distinguishing old signs from new; among readings which attend to the text it cannot be argued that one attends to a truer text than all the others.

It is true that "a fine awareness of human relations," and a certain maturity, may be postulated as classic characteristics; Eliot found them in Virgil. But it is also true that the coexistence in a single text of plurality of significances from which, in the nature of human attentiveness, every reader misses some—and, in the nature of human individuality, prefers one—is, empirically, a requirement and a distinguishing feature of the survivor, *centum qui perfecit annos*. All those little critics, each with his piece to say about *King Lear* or *Wuthering Heights,* may be touched by a venal professional despair, but at least their numbers and their variety serve to testify to the plurality of the documents on which they swarm; and though they may lack authority, sometimes perhaps even sense, many of them do point to what is *there* and ought not to be wished away.

A recognition of this plurality relieves us of the necessity of a *Wuthering Heights* without a Heathcliff, just as it does of a *Wuthering Heights* that "really" ends with the death of Catherine, or for that matter an *Aeneid* which breaks off, as some of the moral allegorists would perhaps have liked it to, at the end of book 6. A reading such as that with which I began [*The Classic: Literary Images of Permanence and Change*] is of course extremely selective, but it has the negative virtue that it does not excommunicate from the text the material it does not employ; indeed, it assumes that it is one of the very large number of readings that may be generated from the text of the novel. They will of course overlap, as mine in some small measure does with that of Mrs. Leavis.

And this brings me to the point: Mrs. Leavis's reading is privileged;

what conforms with it is complex, what does not is confused; and presumably all others would be more or less wrong, in so far as they treated the rejected portions as proper objects of attention. On the other hand, the view I propose does not in any way require me to reject Mrs. Leavis's insights. It supposes that the reader's share in the novel is not so much a matter of knowing, by heroic efforts of intelligence and divination, what Emily Brontë really meant—knowing it, quite in the manner of Schleiermacher, better than she did—as of responding creatively to indeterminacies of meaning inherent in the text and possibly enlarged by the action of time.

We are entering, as you see, a familiar zone of dispute. Mrs. Leavis is rightly concerned with what is "timeless" in the classic, but for her this involves the detection and rejection of what exists, it seems to her irrelevantly or even damagingly, in the aspect of time. She is left, in the end, with something that, in her view, has not changed between the first writing and her reading. I, on the other hand, claimed to be reading a text that might well signify differently to different generations, and different persons within those generations. It is a less attractive view, I see; an encouragement to foolishness, a stick that might be used, quite illicitly as it happens, to beat history, and sever our communications with the dead. But it happens that I set a high value on these, and wish to preserve them. I think there is a substance that prevails, however powerful the agents of change; the *King Lear,* underlying a thousand dispositions, subsists in change, prevails, by being patient of interpretation; that my *Wuthering Heights,* sketchy and provocative as it is, relates as disposition to essence quite as surely as if I had tried to argue that it was Emily Brontë's authorized version, or rather what she intended and could not perfectly execute.

Repression and Sublimation of Nature in *Wuthering Heights*

Margaret Homans

It is a critical commonplace that *Wuthering Heights* is informed by the presence of nature: metaphors drawn from nature provide much of the book's descriptive language—as when Cathy describes Heathcliff as "an arid wilderness of furze and whinstone"—and the reader leaves the book with the sensation of having experienced a realistic portrayal of the Yorkshire landscape. There are, however, very few scenes in the novel that are actually set out-of-doors. With a few exceptions, the crucial events take place in one or the other of the two houses. Cathy and Heathcliff, the characters whose relations to nature would seem to be the strongest and the most important to the novel, are never presented on the moors, together or apart, in either of the two major narrative layers. From their formative childhood we have as evidence of their attachment to nature Cathy's diary account of their naughty escapade under the dairy maid's cloak, but she omits any direct description of what they actually did out-of-doors. In contrast to the lack of detail about Cathy and Heathcliff, the character who is most devoted to staying indoors, Linton Heathcliff, is seen in two extensive outdoor scenes during his meetings with the second Cathy. Cathy both talks about and is seen in nature, but her grand excursion to Penistone Crags, her most significant foray into nature, is left to conjecture. All that is shown of the whole adventure is the encounter inside Wuthering Heights after Nelly arrives.

From *PMLA* 93, no. 1 (January 1978). © 1978 by The Modern Language Association of America. This article has been substantially revised and expanded and comes to different conclusions as "The Name of the Mother in *Wuthering Heights*," chapter 3 of *Bearing the Word: Language and Female Experience in Nineteenth-Century Women's Writing* (The University of Chicago Press, 1986).

It is difficult to catalog something that is not there, but surely it is peculiar that Brontë did not show us even once what her protagonists were like in their element. Heathcliff disappears into a raging storm after hearing Cathy say it would degrade her to marry him. Why does the author not give us one moment's observation of Heathcliff struggling against the storm? There is a brief description of Cathy going out to the road in search of him, "where, heedless of my expostulations, and the growling thunder, and the great drops that began to plash round her, she remained calling, at intervals, and then listening, and then crying outright." But Brontë quickly switches the narrative from Cathy to the scene indoors, so that most of the storm is narrated in terms of how it feels and sounds from inside: the effect of a falling tree limb is measured by the clatter of stones and soot it knocks into the kitchen fire and by Joseph's moralizing vociferations. The next time Cathy enters the narrative she has come back indoors, because the narrative is itself a kind of house, which the characters leave and enter and leave again. Brontë always seems to bend her vision away from nature.

This avoidance of direct presentation of the natural context is caused in part by the chosen perspective of Nelly, who cannot be expected to have followed her characters out into the wilds. She is a "domestic" and her perspective is necessarily housebound. Nelly's indoor perspective would seem to be reinforced by Lockwood's perspective as an invalid in bed during the first part of the narrative and by his displeasure with nature throughout, his own single contact with the elements having been almost lethal. Yet Nelly's narrative has achieved impossibilities elsewhere in the novel, and there is no reason to think that Brontë could not have maneuvered her narrators into position for natural observation if she had wished to do so. She must have had a purpose in choosing two such domestic characters for narrators in the first place.

In a novel whose elaborate structure of narrator-within-narrator puts in doubt the very possibility of talking about a "real" presence of nature or of anything else, it is still necessary to designate a hierarchy of narrative layers according to their relative degrees of realism. The implausible fiction that Nelly spoke her highly literate and structured tale to Lockwood and that Lockwood remembered it and wrote it down verbatim might be evidence for an argument that Brontë is dismissing the current convention of narrative realism. Yet, in spite of this self-proclaiming fictiveness, the novel also makes the effort to maintain the most common attributes of realism: characters that are meant to seem and do seem quite plausible, a cohesive geographical layout, a plot that obeys the laws of cause and effect. The present distinction between the reader's impression of a detailed portrait of

Yorkshire life and landscape and the actual absence of such presentation is itself part of the fine balance Brontë maintains between fictional realism and overt fictiveness. The layering of the narrative enacts the range of degrees of fictiveness. The reader is asked to take Lockwood's account of his own actions and impressions as the most real, since it is the most experiential; Nelly's quoted story would be the next most real, because Lockwood listens to it; but descending from these relatively trustworthy accounts is the hearsay evidence of the various interpolated narratives and letters, which are increasingly further from Lockwood's own experience and liable to greater distortion.

If a narrative scheme were to account only for degrees of narrative realism, then the diary fragment in Cathy's handwriting that Lockwood discovers on a blank page of the Reverend Jabes Branderham's "Seventy Times Seven . . . " would be among the most mediated of narrative layers, distanced as it is by time and by having been accidentally read by, and not spoken to, Lockwood. Yet the descending pattern of realism outlined above is qualified by the fact that Lockwood is also the least reliable narrator, understanding the least, while the interpolated narratives, being increasingly closer to the events themselves, are the most reliable. By this token, the diary fragment is also the most authentic, as well as the most distant, of the narrative layers. It circumvents the complexity of narrative layering, leaping out uncannily to the reader's attention, in spite of the fact that the writer is long dead and her writing is contained between dusty covers. It has the same intrusive effect on the reader that the ghostly Catherine of Lockwood's dream has: it breaks the rules of the narrative scheme just as a ghost breaks the laws of nature. Within the fictive frame of the novel, that is, momentarily allowing the assumption that the events and conversations did take place and that there is somewhere a core of truth from which Lockwood's and Nelly's reports probably swerve, the diary fragment is the only unmediated record of the veritable voice and attitudes of one of the central characters. Isabella's letter to Nelly is another "proof" document, but she is not a central character and her letter is interesting more because it supplies part of the story that Nelly could not have witnessed herself than because it is a sample of a precious voice. The content of the diary fragment is not really important from the point of view of plot, since Nelly later narrates similar episodes from her own recollections. For the rest of the story, the reader must maintain a constant skepticism about the alterations Nelly must have made in the remembered speeches of her characters and also about the alterations Lockwood may have made in his transmission of Nelly's report and in his own remembrances of conversations he himself heard. Written down, and therefore less likely to have been tampered with by Lockwood, Cathy's little testimony of woe rings true, as the closest thing to hearing her speak for herself (although it is admittedly a little disturbing to hear a supposed eleven-year-old using words like "sobriety" and "asseverated"). It is also in the diary fragment that Cathy is introduced in the novel, before the reader meets her in Nelly's narrative, so it touches the reader with a special force of priority.

The fragment serves as an opening statement of the relation between nature and writing in the novel. It is justifiable to take it paradigmatically because it is a diary, as the whole form of the novel is a diary, and, as a written text within a text, it draws attention to itself as writing, in a way that Nelly's spoken story, for example, does not. Like Lockwood's own diary, in which Nelly brings her narrative up to the present time of Lockwood's visit, Cathy starts in the past and writes up to the present time of her writing. But more important than the continuity in time is the significant break in her narrative. After she is caught up to the present she and Heathcliff go for their "scamper on the moors" under the dairy woman's cloak, but this she does not describe. Lockwood leaves a space in his account and then says, "I suppose Catherine fulfilled her project, for the next sentence took up another subject." The adventure takes place in the lacuna. A synecdoche for the narrative as a whole, this little story, like the rest, averts its eyes from nature. Cathy writes nothing about the scamper itself, narrating only what happens indoors, before and after: her anticipation of the event and then, after the gap, her sorrowful reaction to the punishment they receive as a result. The scamper is clearly the preferred alternative to writing: "I have got the time on with writing for twenty minutes; but my companion is impatient and proposes that we should appropriate the dairy woman's cloak, and have a scamper on the moors, under its shelter. A pleasant suggestion." Writing is broken off in favor of action. Further, when Cathy returns to her writing, that action suffices in itself and cannot be improved on by writing it down. Writing is no more than a solace, reserved for hours of boredom, or of loneliness, or of sorrow. Cathy does not write about the scamper itself because writing is stimulated for her only by need, and she needs nothing when she is on the moors. Writing and events in nature are, to the young Cathy, incompatible.

Cathy's omission of any description of the romp on the moors is perfectly in keeping with the pattern of Brontë's own omissions, and, further, it suggests a reason for those omissions. Writing creates an order of priority. Ordinarily, a word presents itself as coming first to the reader, putting its referent in second place. The only way to preserve the priority of something is not to have it named, so that what is primary is just that which is left out of the text, and surely these omissions of descriptions of events in nature are significant holes. Everything else about the diary fragment suggests that nature is primary and that writing is intended to be made secondary. For example, as Lockwood is leafing through the book, Cathy's writing seems at first to be commentary on the printed text, filling out the margins, adding to a text already complete. The caricature of Joseph that precedes the written diary, "rudely yet powerfully sketched," suggests an alternative mode of expression for Cathy's exasperated sense of injustice, indicating in a different way that writing is not primary. She begins writing only because she is caught indoors by the rain and by the fierce sabbath discipline of Hindley and Joseph and must fill up the dreary time because there is nothing else to do. The omission of nature is consistent with this emphasis that nature is primary or original relative to a text, and all the rest of Brontë's omissions make this point too. Both Brontë and her Cathy avoid description of nature or of events in nature because there is no way to name nature without making it secondary. Primary nature neither needs to be nor can be referred to.

The reader becomes accustomed to Brontë's habitual use of the image of the house, with its windows and doors variously locked or open, as a figure for varying psychic conditions—from the locked door that Lockwood encounters on his second visit to Wuthering Heights, where Cathy, Hareton, and Heathcliff are all prisoners of some kind, to the open doors and lattices he finds on his last visit, after the barriers of hatred have broken down between the remaining protagonists. To review this pattern quickly, the closed house generally represents some sort of entrapment: the body as a trap for the soul, as when the window of Heathcliff's room swinging open and letting the rain in signals his death or the flying out of his soul; the entrapment of one character by the will of another, as when Heathcliff locks Nelly and Cathy inside in order to force the marriage with Linton; or the trap of society or convention, as when Cathy remains inside Thrushcross Grange while Heathcliff, expelled, watches from the outside and longs to shatter the great pane of glass that separates them. In view of this symbolic system, the preponderance of scenes taking place indoors and the absence or omission of directly represented natural landscape indicate that the condition of the narrative as a whole is some kind of entrapment too; the author herself feels her creative possibilities limited by an inadequacy in the house of language.

It is important to stress here that Brontë finds language inadequate only for representing nature or events in nature. The diary fragment omits nature, but its portrayal of emotional life, once it has gone indoors, is sophisticated; Cathy's ability to re-create the dramatic scene in the house is just as remarkable as her omission of the scene outdoors. In other regards besides that of representing nature, Brontë's confidence in her rhetorical power is manifest. Most first readers feel that her portrayals of the size and subtlety of the passions exceed all expectation; one senses no limitation there besides that of life itself. She is not disturbed, as writers are today, by the inherent fictiveness of all language. For example, Nelly's first-person narration casts no shadow over the events she narrates; that Brontë dares to give her narrators such specific characters and yet expects her readers to form their own interpretations freely manifests considerable confidence in the objectivity or transparency of language. The limitation of language in regard to nature, while central to the novel, is brought into relief by the lack of limitation in other regards.

Nature is absent from literal presentation, but it is present in figurative language. All language is figurative, as most critics now see it, but there are degrees of figuration just as there are degrees of narrative realism re-sulting from the layering of the narrative. It must be possible to use the term "figurative language" for that which is overtly figurative, as opposed to "literal language," which is only relatively literal, less self-consciously figurative than what is properly called figuration. The idea of nature would have to undergo a radical change in the transition from a posited (but absent) literal sense to a figurative use. There is no literal use of nature because, strictly speaking, to write of it at all is to deny its literalness or primariness, but there is rarely even any relatively literal use of nature, that is, any description of nature for its own sake, without reference to anything outside the immediate scene. The respect for nature's primacy, which this abstention from description implies, is completely bypassed when nature is used for figurative purposes. Nature as a figure becomes subservient to whatever it is used to describe, dropping from the primacy of the unnamed to what might be described as a tertiary status, since it is named not for its own sake but for the sake of something else. This could be called nature as adjective or pronoun, where the place of the noun in such a syntactic model is occupied by the characters who are generally the objects of such figurative descriptions.

To use nature as a figure is to make nature secondary to what it describes, and to describe someone by means of figures—or with language at all—is to impose a limitation of perspectivism or metaphor that reduces whatever is primal in that character. When Heathcliff is "like a savage beast getting goaded to death with knives and spears," both man and beast are brought together into a region of compromise, which impinges on the primacy of each. Heathcliff's agony would seem to be unspeakable, indescribable, so that to reduce that experience to speech is, in some slight way, to diminish its grandeur. The indefinite is sublime; the finite, that which can be figured, is not. Every time the reader's vision of Heathcliff is made definite by a specific comparison, Heathcliff becomes more human and less demonic, even, curiously, when he is compared to a demon. The passages that serve instead to expand the reader's sense of him are those in which the narrator says that some event has been evaded or omitted by the narrative, when a space of absence is opened up, such as his mysterious three-year sojourn or his nighttime wanderings just before his death. Those numinous absences usually take place in unseen nature, just where we have located nature's primacy as well, and have the same status of being primary or original that unseen nature has. There are, then, two radically separate versions of nature in the novel: the primal and literal, which is unseen or evaded, and the figurative, which thrives on the textual surface of the novel.

A characteristic figurative use of nature, often cited as evidence for the presence of "real" nature in the novel, is the device of employing a natural object as a metaphor for character, almost with the force of a metonymy or a symbol, in that frequently the natural object substitutes syntactically for the person described. These are among the most memorable passages in the book not because they introduce "real" nature but because they confirm the reader's sense that the novel is organized by the two opposing principles embodied in the two houses, Wuthering Heights and Thrushcross Grange; they aid the systematization of reading. A brief survey will show that these passages almost always involve a polarity between two extremes, which are implicitly unspeakable unless reduced to a system by natural figures. By taking part in this reductive action nature is similarly reduced: both nature and character serve the ends of comprehensibility. Of Cathy's choice between Linton and Heathcliff Nelly says, "The contrast resembled what you see in exchanging a bleak, hilly, coal country for a beautiful fertile valley." Quickly following this is the related complex of Cathy's own sets of metaphors for her two lovers:

> "Whatever our souls are made of, his and mine are the same, and Linton's is as different as a moonbeam from lightning, or frost from fire."

> "My love for Linton is like the foliage in the woods. Time will change it, I'm well aware, as winter changes the trees. My love for Heathcliff resembles the eternal rocks beneath—a source of little visible delight, but necessary."

Then there is Nelly's description of the relation between Cathy and her new family: "It was not the thorn bending to the honeysuckles, but the honeysuckles embracing the thorn." Culminating the sequence is Cathy's description of Heathcliff's bestiality, though notice that it too hinges on a balancing natural description of Isabella's fragility:

> "Tell her what Heathcliff is—an unreclaimed creature, without refinement, without cultivation; an arid wilderness of furze and whinstone. I'd as soon put that little canary into the park on a winter's day as recommend you to bestow your heart on him! . . . He's not a rough diamond—a pearl-containing oyster of a rustic; he's a fierce, pitiless, wolfish man. . . . He'd crush you, like a sparrow's egg, Isabella, if he found you a troublesome charge."

The disparity between the characteristics of Wuthering Heights and those of the Grange is neatly formulated in opposable natural terms, and those natural symbols center in the part of the book most involved with the tension between the two worlds. Predictably, this kind of description occurs once again and last in a passage about Hareton, in whom the alternatives of the two houses are programmatically combined: "Good things lost amid a wilderness of weeds, to be sure, whose rankness far over-topped their neglected growth; yet notwithstanding, evidence of a wealthy soil that might yield luxuriant crops, under other and favorable circumstances." Heathcliff's furze and Linton's fertile valley combine schematically in the second generation.

These figurative uses of nature, which have always seemed to most readers to bring "real" or unorganized nature into the book, actually provide a vehicle for abstract order. This strategy brings the extremes into an arena of discussion and makes possible relations that might otherwise seem unthinkable. For example, Isabella's attraction to Heathcliff seems extraneous, as "fantastic" to us as it is to Linton, until Cathy's natural metaphors align the axis of their relationship by giving it a basis in the natural law of predator and prey and make it all too logical and comprehensible. Comparisons that intend differentiation actually subvert differentiation, serving to bring two characters closer by furnishing the necessary common ground. Similarly, Cathy means to use rock and foliage, frost and fire, to show herself and Nelly why she believes that her two loves will not impinge on each other (they fulfill two different needs as they exist in two different natural realms); yet by bringing them into such a comparison she also lets the reader, if not herself, discover why such a separation of interests will certainly fail. The natural metaphor is a basis for an interaction that she misunderstands. Any kind of figure would serve as well to bring the unspeakable into the realm of the speakable, but only nature as a source of figures is big enough to act as so effective a ground of mediation.

If natural figures work as a ground for comparisons or alignments that might otherwise not be made at all, it is implied that there must be some ground or point of reference beneath these figures, some generalized sense of "nature" that unifies the individual instances. The impression that the novel gives of depicting the rough Yorkshire landscape and climate is not a wrong one and must come from some source in the novel. This assumed reference might be the same primary nature that is omitted from the diary fragment as from the rest of the narrative, but, if that nature resists naming, it would certainly be separate from any schematization taking place at the textual level. Primal nature remains submerged. Natural figures are instead grounded in another verbal version of nature, symbolic landscapes that are only slightly less figurative than the organizing figures discussed above, in that they appear to be closer to "real" nature and less subservient to the foreground of character. These are landscapes that are described as though they were or could be literally visible but that are as descriptive of the human situation as the more explicit figures are. There remains a gulf between unwritten and written nature.

In the scene just before Heathcliff's return after his long absence, the landscape between the Grange and the Heights hovers on the edge between literal and symbolic description, between degrees of figurativeness. Cathy and Edgar are gazing out at twilight, and, to Nelly, "both the room, and its occupants, and the scene they gazed on looked wondrously peaceful." Yet the action of looking out from inside, which is peaceful, clearly predicts the event to come, almost as though the characters were waiting in expectation. The main feature of the landscape is the "long line of mist," which describes the axis of the two houses but does not quite connect them. The line of mist is on the verge of symbolizing the reconnection of the two houses about to take place, but not quite, because, although the hills called Wuthering Heights rise above the vapor, the house that takes its name from them "was invisible—it rather drops down on the other side." It is a beautiful passage, but it is almost occluded by the requirements of symbolization. The passage intends a vision of repose before the onslaught of Heathcliff's arrival, yet nature is never reposeful because it is always talking, radiating significance. Cathy and Edgar think they are looking out at the unconscious beauty of nature, but they inhabit a text, and the reader knows that they are in the presence of a veritable book of instruction.

This pattern of symbolic landscape continues throughout the novel, and there is a gradual passage from equivocal to unequivocal symbolization. In a passage about nature's obliviousness to Heathcliff's grief over Cathy's death, a symbol for tears lurks in the image of "the dew that had gathered on the budded branches, and fell pattering round him." Four pages later, only hours after Cathy's burial, the spring weather turns to winter and we are back in a fully symbolic landscape. It is no coincidence that the second Cathy's "coming of age," the dreary walk she takes at about the time of her seventeenth birthday when she confronts both her father's coming death and her knowledge of Heathcliff's true evil, is the setting for her discovery of symbolism in a landscape. Thinking of the omission in the other Cathy's diary, one might say that childhood is a time when nature is perceived as itself, with no effort to transform it into a text or to give it any extranatural significance, while adulthood is partly an initiation into symbol making. Nelly points out a last bluebell remaining from summer, under the roots of a tree where Cathy used to climb and sing, "happier than words can express," and suggests that she "clamber up, and pluck it to show papa." Cathy stares at it a long time, then gives it a meaning, as grown-ups would: "No, I'll not touch it—but it looks melancholy, does it not, Ellen?" A little later Cathy and Linton disagree about their ideas of a natural heaven, more or less realizing that nature has become a symbol for character. Toward the end, when Heathcliff's approaching death dominates the narrative, the tendency to render the landscape symbolic is epitomized in his vision of Cathy's spirit in the landscape. He does considerably more than take the landscape as a representation of Cathy, because the landscape is literally replaced by her image: "I cannot look down to this floor, but her features are shaped in the flags! In every cloud, in every tree—filling the air at night, and caught by glimpses in every object, by day I am surrounded with her image!" Days before his death, walking through the house with his eyes focused on a spot a few feet in front of him, Heathcliff seems really to see her ghost and we are asked to believe in a projection, which undoes any remnant sense that the landscape might have qualities of its own. The boy who sees the two ghosts "under t' Nab" after Heathcliff's death verifies the fact that this landscape is saturated not just with the presence of an authorial consciousness but with the human "spirit" as well.

Heathcliff's vision of the world-as-Cathy and the suggestion of ghosts in the landscape are a climax of the tendency toward rendering the landscape symbolic, and they also suggest a further reason for the omissions of scenes of literal or primal nature. We have seen earlier that Brontë does not consider language to be adequate to the task of representing nature, and such representation is neither possible nor desired, but primal nature is textually shunned for another reason as well. The use of nature as a figure and the rendering of highly and increasingly symbolic landscape suggest an active flight away from attempting a (relatively) nonfigurative representation of nature. Why should there be so pronounced a turn? The first encounter with nature in the book is also the closest textual approach to literal nature that Brontë presents. The snowstorm of chapter 3, wholly adversary, all but obliterates both the path back to Thrushcross Grange and Lockwood's health. The path was previously marked by stones daubed with lime, but the storm has covered the ground so deeply that, "excepting a dirty dot pointing up, here and there, all traces of their existence had vanished." Nature is combating the human attempt to make nature legible, and the scarcity of those "dirty dots" causes Lockwood to founder in his reading of nature. After this episode, the narrative veers away from such direct contacts with nature, as if the narrative, which constantly imposes a reading on nature, would suffer as much as Lockwood does. Literal or primary nature, entering the region of consciousness or textuality, is death-dealing. Avoiding literal nature in the novel, Brontë offers instead a tertiary version of nature, which has, in contrast, the life-sustaining qualities of all figuration: figures mark a helpful path around or over rather than through nature, avoiding the dangers of snowstorms. She compares Heathcliff to a wilderness of furze in order not to show him in an actual wilderness, which would be difficult and painful to describe. Figuration lifts her from the ground.

Freud describes repression as a defense mechanism that is turned against instincts, primarily sexual ones. To gratify these instincts would bring immediate pleasure, but it would ultimately bring an even greater degree of unpleasure, because it would call up fresh causes for repression. Literary critics interpret repression to mean an action performed not on sexual instincts but on analogous threats to psychic pleasure or psychic life. In *Poetry and Repression* Harold Bloom tells us that poets must repress their awareness of their debt to literary precursors in order to keep on writing. To oversimplify vastly Bloom's complex argument, this repression occurs because, although capitulation to the greatness of the precursor would solve the immediate painful conflict, it also would bring about the greater displeasure of writing weak poetry or no poetry at all. Jacques Derrida in his article "Freud and the Scene of Writing" gives repression a similarly privileged role in making writing possible. Repression partially breaks the contact between the unconscious or memory and the conscious or perception, so that memory does not block the acquisition of new perceptions, and writing is then the relation, the single point of contact between memory and perception. It is not necessary to go so far as to point to the displacement into nature of either Brontë's libido or her precursors as the cause of her repression of nature. The common characteristic of that which is said to be repressed, whether it be instinct, precursors, or memory, is that it carries the force of literal meaning and thus has primacy, because figuration is a deviation from the literal and is therefore secondary. Instinct, precursors, and memory are involuntary residents of consciousness: that is, if they are part of psychic content it is not because the psyche wills it so. They hinder psychic health, or creativity as a literary form of psychic health, by putting everything that is a product of the will into a secondary position, the position of having deviated from an original. They dominate the claim to primacy. In the case of Brontë, literal nature has the effect of blocking creativity by making her feel that anything she writes about it will be secondary. I am not attempting here to psychoanalyze the biographical Emily Brontë; I am referring to the psyche that is available to the reader, Brontë as she presents herself in the text, intentionally or not. If actual people repress threatening drives by abstaining from those activities, or repress dangerous memories by forgetting them, then the corresponding act of repression for the literary psyche would be to keep the dangerous element out of the text, which is that psyche's version of consciousness. Brontë must repress literal nature by not naming it directly, in order to write.

In Freud, "successful" repression, repression that succeeds in driving the threatening force underground forever, is not as desirable as certain kinds of unsuccessful repression, if the repressed material returns in a different and unthreatening form. This is one of Freud's definitions of sublimation, and that is what Brontë's conversion of literal nature into figuration accomplishes: repressed material returns in a form useful to her, radiantly creative because it has been tamed, made tertiary, deprived of its threatening independence of meaning and subservient to imposed meaning. The energy cathected to one has been transferred to the other. This is why there is an absolute difference between primal nature, whose lurking presence is only implied, and figurative nature, which appears so abundantly: when the repressed material returns, it must be cleared of original or literal meaning. (Sublimation is distinct from reaction-formation, which is the substitution of something harmless for something too potent. Here, sublimation offers an altered version of the same, not a substitution.)

In *The Problem of Anxiety* and *Three Essays on the Theory of Sexuality* Freud proposes a model for sublimation, which may describe the process as it functions in *Wuthering Heights*. An activity that is not inherently erotic can become eroticized and, once it has taken on the force of a sexual drive, the individual will then abstain from it just as if it were actually dangerous. This takes place because of excessive eroticization of the part of the body that performs the activity. Freud's image for this process is the path: a path is broken in the psyche, allowing too great contact between sex and the fingers or writing or between sex and the feet or walking. If the process is one of pathbreaking, then it should be possible to reverse the direction of the path or to travel psychically in the opposite direction, away from rather than toward eroticization. To take this path backward, to desexualize a function in order that it cease to require repression, is to sublimate. On the basis of this model, it could be said that there is a psychic path in Brontë between nature and some primal force, not necessarily sexual, which could be called her sense of the literal, or whatever it is that threatens to preempt her power to write or to imagine. Fearing that it is nature that threatens creativity, she abstains from bringing nature into her novel as an unmediated presence. In Cathy's diary fragment, an experience in nature does not need to be written about, but the reader also suspects it could not be written about. Perhaps Brontë's fear is that, if she were to attempt to write nature directly into her book, the attempt would produce silence, because reality can never enter a text without mediation. Her figurative uses of nature suggest that the path can be and is reversed. Instead of associating nature with the force of the literal, she associates it with that which is purely nonliteral, her invented characters. Nature is deprived of its primacy, or de-eroticized on the Freudian model; yet the sublimation into figure making cannot have redirected all the energy attached to the repressed material— or the path is at best a two-way street—because she still cannot write a scene in nature that does not testify to constant vigilance, and the lacunae show that repression is still at work. In some of the symbolic landscapes we have seen how she verges on affording the image some degree of independence from her characters, but her inability to sustain this for long is the trace of a repression not wholly cured or emptied out.

It is important to point out that she is repressing, not nature, but what nature has come to represent or to be associated with; nature is a vehicle for something else. In one paper on repression Freud makes a distinction between the instinct and its "ideational representative." The repressed itself cannot be named because as such it never enters consciousness at all. Nature does enter consciousness, or the present time of the narrative (in the form of Lockwood's fearful snowstorm), and is then driven out again, to be sublimated later. We must take the nature that is absent from *Wuthering Heights* as the ideational representative of something inherently unnamable, perhaps what we call reality, perhaps something else. What Freud is saying is that a process like sublimation, the process of finding a name for the feared thing, takes place even before repression proper can begin. Repression appears to be directed at the nature that is omitted in Brontë's lacunae, but there is an even more threatening force behind that nature, for which nature is only the representative.

When Cathy is sick with her fatal "madness" she speaks the only direct or scenic presentation in the novel of any part of her and Heathcliff's childhood on the moors. Pulling the feathers out of her pillow, she finds a lapwing's, which looses a flood of memory:

> "Bonny bird; wheeling over our heads in the middle of the moor. It wanted to get to its nest, for the clouds touched the swells, and it felt rain coming. This feather was picked up from the heath, the bird was not shot—we saw its nest in winter, full of little skeletons. Heathcliff set a trap over it, and the old ones dare not come. I made him promise he'd never shoot a lapwing, after that, and he didn't."

The description is made possible by her derangement. Such direct narration of an episode in nature, which amounts to reliving it, is not possible in a healthy state. Even if it were possible, the repression and sublimation of nature in the rest of the novel suggest that such a description could bring on madness. It is the return of repressed material not sublimated into figures but whole, direct, and all at once. It is as though, on the "path" model of the eroticization and subsequent sublimation, or desexualization, of a function, Cathy were dying of her inability to reverse the path. Only nature has become not eroticized (though that may be part of it, in that, in her love for Heathcliff and in her association of Heathcliff with nature, she may have transferred erotic longings to nature), nor is it the ideational representative of what Brontë herself is repressing. For Cathy, nature is dangerous because it is so totally identified with Heathcliff. When she returns from her visit to Thrushcross Grange, her initial reaction of repulsion toward Heathcliff comes from his dirt and his wildness, in other words, from his life as a savage in nature. She has learned, as part of the civilizing influence of the Lintons, that dirt is bad and that therefore her own savage past was bad and that therefore any relic of that past, such as Heathcliff's perennially dirty person, is to be avoided. Nature, Heathcliff, and her former delight in nature are all rejected at once, as a complex of associated repressions. Later, when Heathcliff has come to be the most threatening of those repressed functions, the other two, nature and her memories of the past, are repressed all the more forcefully for their continued association with Heathcliff. The association becomes a representation. During Heath-cliff's absence and her marriage to Linton she successfully repressed her love for Heathcliff, but, when Heathcliff returns, the personification of a repressed instinct bursting through the barriers of her repression, the psychic health of her tranquil life with Linton is destroyed by a resumption of the unresolvable mental strife between her conflicting loves, or rather, more specifically, by the need for a fresh effort of repression. Heathcliff, the past, and nature were repressed together. The return of one brings with it the return of the associated repressions, and the flooding return of the story of the lapwing is evidence that all those barriers have collapsed. During her illness her chief desires are to be outside on the moors and to return to her childhood, without much specific reference to a longing for Heathcliff himself. Those repressed desires might come back harmlessly if they were not still tied to her desire for Heathcliff, if she could reverse the path and undo their association with Heathcliff. But every memory of the past, specifically the lapwing story, undoes her efforts to regain psychic health.

Looking closer at the lapwing story, the reader finds a particular reason for the anxiety caused by memories such as this one that tie nature and Heathcliff together. There is something suspect about the absence of Heath-cliff from her other memories. She fantasizes that she is back at Wuthering Heights, in her own room, and her constant refrain is the wish to be outside on the moors and to be her former self, but the strength-giving recollections that provoke such desires do not seem to include Heathcliff:

> "Oh, if I were but in my own bed in the old house!" she went on bitterly, wringing her hands. "And that wind sounding in the firs by the lattice. Do let me feel it—it comes straight down the moor. . . . I wish I were out of doors—I wish I were a girl again, half savage and hardy, and free. . . . I'm sure I should be myself were I once among the heather on those hills."

Waking from her first fit of unconsciousness, she finds she had forgotten (or repressed) all of her life since the last occasion of being at one with Heathcliff, just before their last expedition to spy in the windows at the Grange, the history of her defection from Heathcliff. Her remembrance of the separation ordered at that time between her and Heathcliff is extremely painful, but the recollected tears are nothing compared to the agony of the fruits of her own willing separation, when memory comes rushing back: "My late anguish was swallowed in a paroxysm of despair." She is por-traying to herself a memory of childhood that now seems relatively idyllic, because its only sorrowful moments came from an external and readily detestable agent. Regression to childhood is her escape from, and refutation of, a difficult adult present that is of her own making. Yet the story about the lapwing feather belies the idealization of her childhood of which Cathy would convince herself. She scans her real memories of childhood and finds a vision that is neither innocent nor curative, but nightmarish. The illogical order of the events in her account shows her mind moving nervously, too quickly, over memory. She should tell about the trap before she tells about the "little skeletons," for example. The setting is the onset of a storm. The episode reveals acutely what the reader suspected but never could verify from previous episodes: that Heathcliff was as sadistic in his relatively happy childhood as he is as an adult. Further, the motif of abandoned infants is a recurrent one. Heathcliff himself was left to starve by his own parents, and, orphaned again by Mr. Earnshaw's death, he was subject to the cruelty of another parent figure. In addition to being cruel, Heathcliff is already a symbol maker, old beyond his years, imposing the horrors of his own experience on a helpless world of things. The picture of the children's experience of nature is hardly as innocent as Cathy might have led herself and the reader to believe, during her outbursts of longing for the past.

The story is also not about Heathcliff alone. The most curious fact about it is Cathy's half-willing complicity in its events. She finds her reward for the painful memory in the recollection of Heathcliff's sweet obedience to her request not to shoot any more lapwings and takes it as evidence of a harmonious childhood. However, her interdict on shooting extends only to lapwings, and, by distinguishing shooting as the form of killing of which she disapproves, she half admits an attraction to the far more perverse technique that Heathcliff did use. Where spots of blood as evidence of shooting would upset her, the trap placed over the nest causes her no special distress; and there is clearly a macabre fascination in the tone of "full of little skeletons," a mixture of attraction and repulsion. After all, if her reaction had been one of complete distaste, she would have made him promise never to kill any birds, or any animals, using whatever weapon. But she does not. The memory, almost blurted out, testifies to why she is really so afraid, to the point of madness. Real memories such as that one, memories that balance Heathcliff's sweet submission with his diabolical cruelty and implicate her in a similar way, preempt her reconstructed memories, which are as secondary as any figure or other deviation from literal truth. Any effort to recreate a nicer childhood and so attain some degree of psychic health for the present is ruined by such influxes of the literal.

It is not Brontë's but her fictional character's repressions that have so disastrously returned. Nature and her memory of the past are Cathy's ideational representatives for Heathcliff, or for that in her which "is" Heathcliff, and that repression is distinct from Brontë's repression. Nevertheless, Cathy's experience must be analogous to Brontë's own. The lapwing story is just such a narrative as we might have expected to find in the part of the book about Cathy and Heathcliff's childhood, and its late appearance, out of sequence, suggests that it functions for Brontë as a return of her own narrative omissions, a return of her own repressed. It is, of course, impossible to know whether Brontë consciously determined this pattern or whether it is truly a welling up of unconscious elements; in either case, the reader's experience is the same. The analogy between Cathy and her creator may help to designate what it is about literal nature that Brontë finds necessary (intentionally or not) to repress. Cathy represses nature as a representative of that in her which "is" Heathcliff, because, like anything that claims primacy in the psyche, it blocks her efforts to reimagine the past. This aspect of the analogy only confirms what the reader already knows about Brontë's avoidance of the literal in order not to let her own writing appear secondary. In this she is successful, because, even though nature is presented almost exclusively in overt figures, those figures give the reader the impression of a much more literal depiction of nature.

Cathy also represses the Heathcliff-nature complex because of the content of that primal memory, as well as because of its effect of primacy. The memory is cruel to her because it is a memory of cruelty, Heathcliff's and her own. The lapwing story shows that love and violence, love and death are identified in him and in the medium of their relationship; it gives her to herself suicidally. Nature, or the literal as it is represented by nature, appears to provoke a similar attitude in Brontë, whether that attitude becomes part of a conscious strategy of writing or remains unconscious. Not only is nature's literality destructive to creative energy, but nature is also literally destructive. Lockwood's snowstorm erases nature's readability, but, beyond that, nearly kills that reader, Lockwood, himself. To try to name literal nature in the novel after that, aside from the technical difficulty of doing so, would make it necessary to inflict harm on her characters in addition to the harm they do to each other. Nature, or "reality," just like Heathcliff in Cathy's memory, cuts off relations between parents and children, between those who love one another, and causes distress, starvation, and death. Nature's truth is death, and only when reimagined does it approach neutrality or beneficence.

The lapwing story, paired with the fragment of Cathy's diary, also presents an alternative paradigm for the relation between nature and writing.

The diary omits an episode in nature, for the sake of not distorting nature, and the primary experience of nature, with inadequate language, while Cathy's madness produces a story that distorts her psychic health. The two stories are paradigms for narrative options or poles at the extremes of a narrative axis: blank spaces at one end and confused, fevered talk at the other. That Brontë creates a large figure for her own repressed condition, as well as making constructive figurative language out of the repressed material itself, shows that figuration is her best outlet for repression. But the difference between herself and Cathy, the eccentricity in the analogy, gives her even more than does the initial similarity. If the analogy to the diary fragment were carried out fully, then, in addition to drawing inferences from what Cathy leaves out, we would be obliged to take as a paradigm what Cathy does write about and to suggest that Brontë, too, writes as a solace for moments of solitude or sorrow. That would produce a reductive theory of therapeutic writing, which is certainly not applicable to so powerful a novelist. Similarly, the analogy drawn from the lapwing story would lead to a theory of passive or stream-of-consciousness writing or to a theory identifying fiction with dreams. Brontë can reverse the psychic path and avoid the extremes of Cathy's condition, and the diary and the lapwing story are there to admonish and to mark outer limits, rather than to provide exactly tailored paradigms. Making the figures is only part of the process of recovery; surpassing them is even better. To be tied down to a figure would only be to instigate a new cause for repression.

Looking Oppositely:
Catherine Earnshaw's Fall

Sandra M. Gilbert

Because Emily Brontë was looking oppositely not only for heaven (and hell) but for her own female origins, *Wuthering Heights* is one of the few authentic instances of novelistic mythmaking, mythmaking in the functional sense of problem-solving. Where writers from Charlotte Brontë and Henry James to James Joyce and Virginia Woolf have used mythic material to give point and structure to their novels, Emily Brontë uses the novel form to give substance—plausibility, really—to her myth. It is urgent that she do so because, as we shall see, the feminist cogency of this myth derives not only from its daring corrections of Milton but also from the fact that it is a distinctively nineteenth-century answer to the question of origins: it is the myth of how culture came about, and specifically of how nineteenth-century society occurred, the tale of where tea-tables, sofas, crinolines, and parsonages like the one at Haworth came from.

Because it is so ambitious a myth, *Wuthering Heights* has the puzzling self-containment of a *mystery* in the old sense of that word—the sense of mystery plays and Eleusinian mysteries. Locked in by Lockwood's uncomprehending narrative, Nelly Dean's story, with its baffling duplication of names, places, events, seems endlessly to reenact itself, like some ritual that must be cyclically repeated in order to sustain (as well as explain) both nature and culture. At the same time, because it is so prosaic a myth—a myth about crinolines!—*Wuthering Heights* is not in the least portentous or self-consciously "mythic." On the contrary, like all true rituals and myths,

From *The Madwoman in the Attic: The Woman Writer and the Nineteenth-Century Literary Imagination.* © 1979 by Yale University. Yale University Press, 1979.

Brontë's "cuckoo's tale" turns a practical, casual, humorous face to its audience. For as Lévi-Strauss's observations suggest, true believers gossip by the prayer wheel, since that modern reverence which enjoins solemnity is simply the foster child of modern skepticism.

Gossipy but unconventional true believers were rare, even in the pious nineteenth century, as Arnold's anxious meditations and Carlyle's angry sermons note. But Brontë's paradoxically matter-of-fact imaginative strength, her ability to enter a realistically freckled fantasy land, manifested itself early. One of her most famous adolescent diary papers juxtaposes a plea for culinary help from the parsonage housekeeper, Tabby—"Come Anne pilloputate"—with "The Gondals are discovering the interior of Gaaldine" and "Sally Mosely is washing in the back kitchen." Significantly, no distinction is made between the heroic exploits of the fictional Gondals and Sally Mosely's real washday business. The curiously childlike voice of the diarist records all events without commentary, and this reserve suggests an implicit acquiescence in the equal "truth" of all events. Eleven years later, when the sixteen-year-old reporter of "pilloputate" has grown up and is on the edge of *Wuthering Heights,* the naive, uninflected surface of her diary papers is unchanged:

> Anne and I went our first long journey by ourselves together, leaving home on the 30th of June, Monday, sleeping at York, returning to Keighley Tuesday evening . . . during our excursion we were Ronald Mcalgin, Henry Angora, Juliet Angusteena, Rosabella Esmalden, Ella and Julian Egremont, Catharine Navarre, and Cordilia Fitzaphnold, escaping from the palaces of instruction to join the Royalists who are hard driven at present by the victorious Republicans. . . . I must hurry off now to my turning and ironing. I have plenty of work on hands, and writing, and am altogether full of business.

Psychodramatic "play," this passage suggests, is an activity at once as necessary and as ordinary as housework: ironing and the exploration of alternative lives are the same kind of "business"—a perhaps uniquely female idea of which Anne Bradstreet and Emily Dickinson, those other visionary housekeepers, would have approved.

No doubt, however, it is this deep-seated tendency of Brontë's to live literally with the fantastic that accounts for much of the critical disputation about *Wuthering Heights,* especially the quarrels about the novel's genre and style. Q. D. Leavis and Arnold Kettle, for instance, insist that the work is a "sociological novel," while Mark Schorer thinks it "means to be a work of edification [about] the nature of a grand passion." Leo Bersani sees it as an ontological psychodrama, and Elliot Gose as a sort of expanded fairy tale. And strangely there is truth in all these apparently conflicting notions, just as it is also true that (as Robert Kiely has affirmed) "part of the distinction of *Wuthering Heights* [is] that it has no 'literary' aura about it," and true at the same time that (as we have asserted) *Wuthering Heights* is an unusually literary novel because Brontë approached reality chiefly through the mediating agency of literature. In fact, Kiely's comment illuminates not only the uninflected surface of the diary papers but also the controversies about their author's novel, for Brontë is "unliterary" in being without a received sense of what the eighteenth century called literary decorum. As one of her better-known poems declares, she follows "where [her] own nature would be leading," and that nature leads her to an oddly literal— and also, therefore, unliterary—use of extraordinarily various literary works, ideas, and genres, all of which she refers back to herself, since "it vexes [her] to choose another guide."

Thus *Wuthering Heights* is in one sense an elaborate gloss on the Byronic Romanticism and incest fantasy of *Manfred,* written, as Ratchford suggested, from a consciously female perspective. Heathcliff's passionate invocations of Catherine ("Come in! . . . hear me" [chap. 3] or "Be with me always— take any form—drive me mad" [chap. 16] almost exactly echo Manfred's famous speech to Astarte ("Hear me, hear me . . . speak to me! Though it be in wrath . . . "). In another way, though, *Wuthering Heights* is a prose redaction of the metaphysical storms and ontological nature/culture conflicts embodied in *King Lear,* with Heathcliff taking the part of Nature's bastard son Edmund, Edgar Linton incarnating the cultivated morality of his namesake Edgar, and the "wuthering" chaos at the Heights repeating the disorder that overwhelms Lear's kingdom when he relinquishes his patriarchal control to his diabolical daughters. But again, both poetic Byronic Romanticism and dramatic Shakespearean metaphysics are filtered through a novelistic sensibility with a surprisingly Austenian grasp of social details, so that *Wuthering Heights* seems also, in its "unliterary" way, to reiterate the feminist psychological concerns of a *bildungsroman* Brontë may never have read: Jane Austen's *Northanger Abbey.* Catherine Earnshaw's "half savage and hardy and free" girlhood, for example, recalls the tomboy childhood of that other Catherine, Catherine Morland, and Catherine Earnshaw's fall into ladylike "grace" seems to explore the tragic underside of the anxiously comic initiation rites Catherine Morland undergoes at Bath and at Northanger Abbey.

The world of *Wuthering Heights,* in other words, like the world of

Brontë's diary papers, is one where what seem to be the most unlikely opposites coexist without, apparently, any consciousness on the author's part that there is anything unlikely in their coexistence. The ghosts of Byron, Shakespeare, and Jane Austen haunt the same ground. People with decent Christian names (Catherine, Nelly, Edgar, Isabella) inhabit a landscape in which also dwell people with strange animal or nature names (Hindley, Hareton, Heathcliff). Fairy-tale events out of what Mircea Eliade would call "great time" are given a local habitation and a real chronology in just that historical present Eliade defines as great time's opposite. Dogs and gods (or goddesses) turn out to be not opposites but, figuratively speaking, the same words spelled in different ways. Funerals are weddings, weddings, funerals. And of course, most important for our purposes here, hell is heaven, heaven, hell, though the two are not separated, as Milton and literary decorum would prescribe, by vast eons of space but by a little strip of turf, for Brontë was rebelliously determined to walk

> not in old heroic traces
> And not in paths of high morality.
> And not among the half-distinguished faces,
> The clouded forms of long-past history.

On the contrary, surveying that history and its implications, she came to the revisionary conclusion that "the earth that wakes *one* human heart to feeling / Can centre both worlds of Heaven and Hell."

If we identify with Lockwood, civilized man at his most genteelly "cooked" and literary, we cannot fail to begin Brontë's novel by deciding that hell is a household very like Wuthering Heights. Lockwood himself, as if wittily predicting the reversal of values that is to be the story's central concern, at first calls the place "a perfect misanthropist's Heaven" (chap. 1). But then what is the traditional Miltonic or Dantesque hell if not a misanthropist's heaven, a site that substitutes hate for love, violence for peace, death for life, and in consequence the material for the spiritual, disorder for order? Certainly Wuthering Heights rings all these changes on Lockwood's first two visits. Heathcliff's first invitation to enter, for instance, is uttered through closed teeth, and appropriately enough it seems to his visitor to express "the sentiment 'Go to the Deuce.' " The house's other inhabitants—Catherine II, Hareton, Joseph, and Zillah, as we later learn—are for the most part equally hostile on both occasions, with Joseph muttering insults, Hareton surly, and Catherine II actually practicing (or pretending to practice) the "black arts." Their energies of hatred, moreover, are directed not only at their uninvited guest but at each other, as Lockwood learns to his sorrow when Catherine II suggests that Hareton should accompany him through the storm and Hareton refuses to do so if it would please *her*.

The general air of sour hatred that blankets the Heights, moreover, manifests itself in a continual, aimless violence, a violence most particularly embodied in the snarling dogs that inhabit the premises. "In an arch under the dresser," Lockwood notes, "reposed a huge, liver-coloured bitch pointer, surrounded by a swarm of squealing puppies; and other dogs haunted other recesses" (chap. 1). His use of *haunted* is apt, for these animals, as he later remarks, are more like "four-footed fiends" than ordinary canines, and in particular Juno, the matriarch of the "hive," seems to be a parody of Milton's grotesquely maternal Sin, with her yapping brood of hellhounds. Significantly, too, the only nonhostile creatures in this fiercely satanic stronghold are dead: in one of a series of blackly comic blunders, Lockwood compliments Catherine II on what in his decorous way he assumes are her cats, only to learn that the "cats" are just a heap of dead rabbits. In addition, though the kitchen is separate from the central family room, "a vast oak dresser" reaching "to the very roof" of the sitting room is laden with oatcakes, guns, and raw meat: "clusters of legs of beef, mutton, and ham." Dead or raw flesh and the instruments by which living bodies may be converted into more dead flesh are such distinctive features of the room that even the piles of oatcakes and the "immense pewter dishes . . . towering row after row" (chap. 1) suggest that, like hell or the land at the top of the beanstalk, Wuthering Heights is the abode of some particularly bloodthirsty giant.

The disorder that quite naturally accompanies the hatred, violence, and death that prevail at Wuthering Heights on Lockwood's first visits leads to more of the city-bred gentleman's blunders, in particular his inability to fathom the relationships among the three principal members of the household's pseudo-family—Catherine II, Hareton, and Heathcliff. First he suggests that the girl is Heathcliff's "amiable lady," then surmises that Hareton is "the favoured possessor of the beneficent fairy" (chap. 2). His phrases, like most of his assumptions, parody the sentimentality of fictions that keep women in their "place" by defining them as beneficent fairies or amiable ladies. Heathcliff, perceiving this, adds a third stereotype to the discussion: "You would intimate that [my wife's] spirit has taken the form of ministering angel," he comments with the "almost diabolical sneer" of a satanic literary critic. But of course, though Lockwood's thinking is stereotypical, he is right to expect some familial relationship among his tea-table companions, and right too to be daunted by the hellish lack of relationship among them. For though Hareton, Heathcliff, and Catherine II are all in some sense related, the primordial schisms that have overwhelmed the Heights with hatred and violence have divided them from the human orderliness represented by the ties of kinship. Thus just as Milton's hell consists of envious and (in the poet's view) equality-mad devils jostling for position, so these inhabitants of Wuthering Heights seem to live in chaos without the structuring principle of heaven's hierarchical chain of being, and therefore with the heavenly harmony God the Father's ranking of virtues, thrones, and powers makes possible. For this reason Catherine sullenly refuses to do anything "except what I please" (chap. 4), the servant Zillah vociferously rebukes Hareton for laughing, and old Joseph—whose viciously parodic religion seems here to represent a hellish joke at heaven's expense—lets the dogs loose on Linton without consulting his "maister," Heathcliff.

In keeping with this problem of "equality," a final and perhaps definitive sign of the hellishness that has enveloped Wuthering Heights at the time of Lockwood's first visits is the blinding snowfall that temporarily imprisons the by now unwilling guest in the home of his infernal hosts. Pathless as the kingdom of the damned, the "billowy white ocean" of cold that surrounds Wuthering Heights recalls the freezing polar sea on which Frankenstein, Walton, the monster—and the Ancient Mariner—voyaged. It recalls, too, the "deep snow and ice" of Milton's hell, "A gulf profound as that *Serbonian* Bog . . . Where Armies whole have sunk" and where "by harpy-footed" and no doubt rather Heathcliff-ish "Furies hal'd / . . . all the damn'd / Are brought . . . to starve in Ice" (*Paradise Lost* 2.592–600). But of course, as *King Lear* implies, hell is simply another word for uncontrolled "nature," and here as elsewhere *Wuthering Heights* follows *Lear's* model.

Engulfing the Earnshaws' ancestral home and the Linton's, too, in a blizzard of destruction, hellish nature traps and freezes everyone in the isolation of a "perfect misanthropist's heaven." And again, as in *Lear* this hellish nature is somehow female or associated with femaleness, like an angry goddess shaking locks of ice and introducing Lockwood (and his readers) to the female rage that will be a central theme in *Wuthering Heights*. The femaleness of this "natural" hell is suggested, too, by its likeness to the "false" material creation Robert Graves analyzed so well in *The White Goddess*. Female nature has risen, it seems, in a storm of protest, just as the Sin-like dog Juno rises in a fury when Lockwood "unfortunately indulge[s] in winking and making faces" at her while musing on his heartless treatment of a "goddess" to whom he never "told" his love (chap. 1). Finally, that the storm is both hellish and female is made clearest of all by Lockwood's second visionary dream. Out of the tapping of branches, out of the wind and swirling snow, like an icy-fingered incarnation of the storm rising in protest against the patriarchal sermon of "Jabes Branderham," appears that ghostly female witch-child the *original* Catherine Earnshaw, who has now been "a waif for twenty years."

Why is Wuthering Heights so Miltonically hellish? And what happened to Catherine Earnshaw? Why has she become a demonic, storm-driven ghost? The "real" etiological story of *Wuthering Heights* begins, as Lockwood learns from his "human fixture" Nelly Dean, with a random weakening of the fabric of ordinary human society. Once upon a time, somewhere in what mythically speaking qualifies as pre-history or what Eliade calls "illo tempore," there is/was a primordial family, the Earnshaws, who trace their lineage back at least as far as the paradigmatic Renaissance inscription "1500 Hareton Earnshaw" over their "principal doorway." And one fine summer morning toward the end of the eighteenth century, the "old master" of the house decides to take a walking tour of sixty miles to Liverpool (chap. 4). His decision, like Lear's decision to divide his kingdom, is apparently quite arbitrary, one of those mystifying psychic *données* for which the fictional convention of "once upon a time" was devised. Perhaps it means, like Lear's action, that he is half-consciously beginning to prepare for death. In any case, his ritual questions to his two children—an older son and a younger daughter—and to their servant Nelly are equally stylized and arbitrary, as are the children's answers. "What shall I bring you?" the old master asks, like the fisherman to whom the flounder gave three wishes. And the children reply, as convention dictates, by requesting their heart's desires. In other words, they reveal their true selves, just as a father contemplating his own ultimate absence from their lives might have hoped they would.

Strangely enough, however, only the servant Nelly's heart's desire is sensible and conventional: she asks for (or, rather, accepts the promise of) a pocketful of apples and pears. Hindley, on the other hand, the son who is destined to be next master of the household, does not ask for a particularly masterful gift. His wish, indeed, seems frivolous in the context of the harsh world of the Heights. He asks for a fiddle, betraying both a secret, softhearted desire for culture and an almost decadent lack of virile purpose. Stranger still is Catherine's wish for a whip. "She could ride any horse in the stable," says Nelly, but in the fairy-tale context of this narrative that realistic explanation hardly seems to suffice, for, symbolically, the small Catherine's longing for a whip seems like a powerless younger daughter's yearning for power.

Of course, as we might expect from our experience of fairy tales, at least one of the children receives the desired boon. Catherine gets her whip. She gets it figuratively—in the form of a "gypsy brat"—rather than literally, but nevertheless "it" (both whip and brat) functions just as she must unconsciously have hoped it would, smashing her rival-brother's fiddle and making a desirable third among the children in the family so as to insulate her from the pressure of her brother's domination. (That there should always have been three children in the family is clear from the way other fairy-tale rituals of three are observed, and also from the fact that Heathcliff is given the name of a dead son, perhaps even the true oldest son, as if he were a reincarnation of the lost child.)

Having received her deeply desired whip, Catherine now achieves, as J. Hillis Miller and Leo Bersani have noticed, an extraordinary fullness of being. The phrase may seem pretentiously metaphysical (certainly critics like Q. D. Leavis have objected to such phrases on those grounds) but in discussing the early paradise from which Catherine and Heathcliff eventually fall we are trying to describe elusive psychic states, just as we would in discussing Wordsworth's visionary childhood, Frankenstein's youth before he "learned" that he was (the creator of) a monster, or even the prelapsarian sexuality of Milton's Adam and Eve. And so, like Freud who was driven to grope among such words as *oceanic* when he tried to explain the heaven that lies about us in our infancy, we are obligated to use the paradoxical and metaphorical language of mysticism: phrases like *wholeness, fullness of being,* and *androgyny* come inevitably to mind. All three, as we shall see, apply to Catherine, or more precisely to Catherine-Heathcliff.

In part Catherine's new wholeness results from a very practical shift in family dynamics. Heathcliff as a fantasy replacement of the dead oldest brother does in fact supplant Hindley in the old master's affections, and therefore he functions as a tool of the dispossessed younger sister whose "whip" he is. Specifically, he enables her for the first time to get possession of the kingdom of Wuthering Heights, which under her rule threatens to become, like Gondal, a queendom. In addition to this, however, Heathcliff's presence gives the girl a fullness of being that goes beyond power in household politics, because as Catherine's whip he is (and she herself recognizes this) an alternative self or double for her, a complementary addition to her being who fleshes out all her lacks the way a bandage might staunch a wound. Thus in her union with him she becomes, like Manfred in his union with his sister Astarte, a perfect androgyne. As devoid of sexual awareness as Adam and Eve were in the prelapsarian garden, she sleeps with her whip, her other half, every night in the primordial fashion of the countryside. Gifted with that innocent, unselfconscious sexual energy which Blake saw as eternal delight, she has "ways with her," according to Nelly, "such as I never saw a child take up before" (chap. 5). And if Heathcliff's is the body that does her will—strong, dark, proud, and a native speaker of "gibberish" rather than English—she herself is an "unfeminine" instance of transcendently vital spirit. For she is never docile, never submissive, never ladylike. On the contrary, her joy—and the Coleridgean word is not too strong—is in what Milton's Eve is never allowed: a tongue "always going—singing, laughing, and plaguing everybody who would not do the same," and "ready words: turning Joseph's religious curses into ridicule . . . and doing just what her father hated most" (chap. 5).

Perverse as it may seem, this paradise into which Heathcliff's advent has transformed Wuthering Heights for the young Catherine is as authentic a fantasy for women as Milton's Eden was for men, though Milton's misogynistically cowed daughters have rarely had the revisionary courage to spell out so many of the terms of their dream. Still, that the historical process does yield moments when that feminist dream of wholeness has real consequences is another point Brontë wishes us to consider, just as she wishes to convey her rueful awareness that, given the prior strength of patriarchal misogyny, those consequences may be painful as well as paradisal. Producing Heathcliff from beneath his greatcoat as if enacting a mock birth, old Mr. Earnshaw notes at once the equivocal nature of Catherine's whip: "You must e'en take it as a gift of God, though it's as dark almost as if it came from the devil" (chap. 4). His ambivalence is well-founded: strengthened by Heathcliff, Catherine becomes increasingly rebellious against the parodic patriarchal religion Joseph advocates, and thus, too, increasingly unmindful of her father's discipline. As she gains in rebellious energy, she becomes satanically "as Gods" in her defiance of such socially constituted authority, and in the end, like a demonic Cordelia (that is, like Cordelia, Goneril, and Regan all in one) she has the last laugh at her father, answering his crucial dying question "Why canst thou not always be a good lass, Cathy?" with a defiantly honest question of her own: "Why cannot you always be a good man, Father?" (chap. 5) and then singing him, rather hostilely, "to sleep"—that is, to death.

Catherine's heaven, in other words, is very much like the place such a representative gentleman as Lockwood would call hell, for it is associated (like the hell of *King Lear*) with an ascendent self-willed female who radiates what, as Blake observed, most people consider "diabolical" energy—the creative energy of Los and Satan, the life energy of fierce, raw, uncultivated being. But the ambiguity Catherine's own father perceives in his "gift of God" to the girl is also manifested in the fact that even some of the authentically hellish qualities Lockwood found at Wuthering Heights on his first two visits, especially the qualities of "hate" (i.e., defiance) and "violence" (i.e. energy), would have seemed to him to characterize the Wuthering Heights of Catherine's heavenly childhood. For Catherine, however, the defiance that might seem like hate was made possible by love (her oneness with Heathcliff) and the energy that seemed like violence was facilitated by the peace (the wholeness) of an undivided self.

Nevertheless, her personal heaven is surrounded, like Milton's Eden, by threats from what she would define as "hell." If, for instance, she had in some part of herself hoped that her father's death would ease the stress of that shadowy patriarchal yoke which was the only cloud on her heaven's horizon, Catherine was mistaken. For paradoxically old Earnshaw's passing brings with it the end to Catherine's Edenic "half savage and hardy and free" girlhood. It brings about a divided world in which the once-androgynous child is to be "laid alone" for the first time. And most important it brings about the accession to power of Hindley, by the patriarchal laws of primogeniture the real heir and thus the new father who is to introduce into the novel the proximate causes of Catherine's (and Heathcliff's) fall and subsequent decline.

Catherine's sojourn in the earthly paradise of childhood lasts for six years, according to C. P. Sanger's precisely worked-out chronology, but it takes Nelly Dean barely fifteen minutes to relate the episode. Prelapsarian history, as Milton knew, is easy to summarize. Since happiness has few of the variations of despair, to be unfallen is to be static, whereas to fall is to enter the processes of time. Thus Nelly's account of Catherine's fall takes at least several hours, though it also covers six years. And as she describes it, that fall—or process of falling—begins with Hindley's marriage, an event associated for obvious reasons with the young man's inheritance of his father's power and position.

It is odd that Hindley's marriage should precipitate Catherine out of her early heaven because that event installs an adult woman in the small Heights family circle for the first time since the death of Mrs. Earnshaw four years earlier, and as conventional (or even feminist) wisdom would have it, Catherine "needs" a mother-figure to look after her, especially now that she is on the verge of adolescence. But precisely because she and Heathcliff are twelve years old and growing up, the arrival of Frances is the worst thing that could happen to her. For Frances, as Nelly's narrative indicates, is a model young lady, a creature of a species Catherine, safely sequestered in her idiosyncratic Eden, has had as little chance of encountering as Eve had of meeting a talking serpent before the time came for her to fall.

Of course, Frances is no serpent. On the contrary, light-footed and fresh-complexioned, she seems much more like a late eighteenth-century model of the Victorian angel in the house, and certainly her effect upon Hindley has been both to subdue him and to make him more ethereal. "He had grown sparer, and lost his colour, and spoke and dressed quite differently," Nelly notes (chap. 6); he even proposes to convert one room into a parlor, an amenity Wuthering Heights has never had. Hindley has in fact become a cultured man, so that in gaining a ladylike bride he has, as it were, gained the metaphorical fiddle that was his heart's desire when he was a boy.

It is no doubt inevitable that Hindley's fiddle and Catherine's whip cannot peaceably coexist. Certainly the early smashing of the fiddle by the "whip" hinted at such a problem, and so perhaps it would not be entirely frivolous to think of the troubles that now ensue for Catherine and Heathcliff as the fiddle's revenge. But even without pressing this conceit we can see that Hindley's angel/fiddle is a problematical representative of what is now introduced as the "heavenly" realm of culture. For one thing, her ladylike sweetness is only skin-deep. Leo Bersani remarks that the distinction between the children at the Heights and those at the Grange is the difference between "aggressively selfish children" and "whiningly selfish children." If this is so, Frances foreshadows the children at the Grange—the children of genteel culture—since "her affection [toward Catherine] tired very soon [and] she grew peevish," at which point the now gentlemanly Hindley becomes "tyrannical" in just the way his position as the household's new *pater familias* encourages him to be. His tyranny consists, among other things, in his attempt to impose what Blake would call a Urizenic heavenly order at the heretofore anti-hierarchical Heights. The servants Nelly and Joseph, he decrees, must know their place—which is "the back kitchen"—and Heathcliff, because he is socially nobody, must be exiled from culture: deprived of "the instruction of the curate" and cast out into "the fields" (chap. 6).

Frances's peevishness, however, is not just a sign that her ladylike ways are inimical to the prelapsarian world of Catherine's childhood; it is also a sign that, as the twelve-year-old girl must perceive it, to be a lady is to be diseased. As Nelly hints, Frances is tubercular, and any mention of death causes her to act "half silly," as if in some part of herself she knows she is doomed, or as if she is already half a ghost. And she is. As a metaphor, Frances's tuberculosis means that she is in an advanced state of just that *social* "consumption" which will eventually kill Catherine, too, so that the thin and silly bride functions for the younger girl as a sort of premonition or ghost of what she herself will become.

But of course the social disease of ladyhood, with its attendant silliness or madness, is only one of the threats Frances incarnates for twelve-year-old Catherine. Another, perhaps even more sinister because harder to confront, is associated with the fact that though Catherine may well need a mother—in the sense in which Eve or Mary Shelley's monster needed a mother/model—Frances does not and cannot function as a good mother for her. The original Earnshaws were shadowy but mythically grand, like the primordial "true" parents of fairy tales (or like most parents seen through the eyes of preadolescent children). Hindley and Frances, on the other hand, the new Earnshaws, are troublesomely real though as oppressive as the stepparents in fairy tales. To say that they are in some way like stepparents, however, is to say that they seem to Catherine like transformed or alien parents, and since this is as much a function of her own vision as of the older couple's behavior, we must assume that it has something to do with the changes wrought by the girl's entrance into adolescence.

Why do parents begin to seem like stepparents when their children reach puberty? The ubiquitousness of stepparents in fairy tales dealing with the crises of adolescence suggests that the phenomenon is both deep-seated and widespread. One explanation—and the one that surely accounts for Catherine Earnshaw's experience—is that when the child gets old enough to become conscious of her parents as sexual beings they really do begin to seem like fiercer, perhaps even (as in the case of Hindley and Frances) younger versions of their "original" selves. Certainly they begin to be more threatening (that is, more "peevish" and "tyrannical") if only because the child's own sexual awakening disturbs them almost as much as their sexuality, now truly comprehended, bothers the child. Thus the crucial passage from Catherine's diary which Lockwood reads even before Nelly begins her narration is concerned not just with Joseph's pious oppressions but with the cause of those puritanical onslaughts, the fact that she and Heathcliff must shiver in the garret because "Hindley and his wife [are basking] downstairs before a comfortable fire . . . kissing and talking nonsense by the hour—foolish palaver we should be ashamed of." Catherine's defensiveness is clear. She (and Heathcliff) are troubled by the billing and cooing of her "stepparents" because she understands, perhaps for the first time, the sexual nature of what a minute later she calls Hindley's "paradise on the hearth" and—worse—understands its relevance to her.

Flung into the kitchen, "where Joseph asseverated, 'owd Nick' would fetch us," Catherine and Heathcliff each seek "a separate nook to await his advent." For Catherine-and-Heathcliff—that is, Catherine and Catherine, or Catherine and her whip—have already been separated from each other, not just by tyrannical Hindley, the *deus* produced by time's *machina,* but by the emergence of Catherine's own sexuality, with all the terrors which attend that phenomenon in a puritanical and patriarchal society. And just as peevish Frances incarnates the social illness of ladyhood, so also she quite literally embodies the fearful as well as the frivolous consequences of sexuality. Her foolish if paradisaical palaver on the hearth, after all, leads straight to the death her earlier ghostliness and silliness had predicted. Her sexuality's destructiveness was even implied by the minor but vicious acts of injustice with which it was associated—arbitrarily pulling Heathcliff's hair, for instance—but the sex-death equation, with which Milton and Mary Shelley were also concerned, really surfaces when Frances's and Hindley's son, Hareton, is born. At that time, Kenneth, the lugubrious physician who functions like a medical Greek chorus throughout *Wuthering Heights,* informs Hindley that the winter will "probably finish" Frances.

To Catherine, however, it must appear that the murderous agent is not winter but . . x, for as she is beginning to learn, the Miltonic testaments of her world have told woman that "thy sorrow I will greatly multiply / By thy Conception" (*Paradise Lost* 10.192–95) and the maternal image of Sin birthing Death reinforces this point. That Frances's decline and death accompany Catherine's fall is metaphysically appropriate, therefore. And it is dramatically appropriate as well, for Frances's fate foreshadows the catastrophes which will follow Catherine's fall into sexuality just as surely as the appearance of Sin and Death on earth followed Eve's fall. That Frances's death also, incidentally, yields Hareton—the truest scion of the Earnshaw clan—is also profoundly appropriate. For Hareton is, after all, a resurrected version of the original patriarch whose name is written over the great main door of the house, amid a "wilderness of shameless little boys." Thus his birth marks the beginning of the historical as well as the psychological decline and fall of that satanic female principle which has temporarily usurped his "rightful" place at Wuthering Heights.

Catherine's fall, however, is caused by a patriarchal past and present, besides being associated with a patriarchal future. It is significant, then, that her problems begin—violently enough—when she literally falls down and is bitten by a male bulldog, a sort of guard/god from Thrushcross Grange. Though many readers overlook this point, Catherine does not *go* to the Grange when she is twelve years old. On the contrary, the Grange seizes her and "holds [her] fast," a metaphoric action which emphasizes the turbulent and inexorable nature of the psychosexual *rites de passage Wuthering Heights* describes, just as the ferociously masculine bull/dog—as a symbolic representative of Thrushcross Grange—contrasts strikingly with the ascendancy at the Heights of the hellish female bitch goddess alternately referred to as "Madam" and "Juno."

Realistically speaking, Catherine and Heathcliff have been driven in the direction of Thrushcross Grange by their own desire to escape not only the pietistic tortures Joseph inflicts but also, more urgently, just that sexual awareness irritatingly imposed by Hindley's romantic paradise. Neither sexuality nor its consequences can be evaded, however, and the farther the children run the closer they come to the very fate they secretly wish to avoid. Racing "from the top of the Heights to the park without stopping," they plunge from the periphery of Hindley's paradise (which was transforming their heaven into a hell) to the boundaries of a place that at first seems authentically heavenly, a place full of light and softness and color, a "splendid place carpeted with crimson . . . and [with] a pure white ceiling bordered by gold, a shower of glass-drops hanging in silver chains from the centre, and shimmering with little soft tapers" (chap. 6). Looking in the window, the outcasts speculate that if they were inside such a room "we should have thought ourselves in heaven!" From the outside, at least, the Lintons' elegant haven appears paradisaical. But once the children have experienced its Urizenic interior, they know that in their terms this heaven is hell.

Because the first emissary of this heaven who greets them is the bulldog Skulker, a sort of hellhound posing as a hound of heaven, the wound this almost totemic animal inflicts upon Catherine is as symbolically suggestive as his role in the girl's forced passage from Wuthering Heights to Thrushcross Grange. Barefoot, as if to emphasize her "wild child" innocence, Catherine is exceptionally vulnerable, as a wild child must inevitably be, and when the dog is "throttled off, his huge, purple tongue hanging half a foot out of his mouth . . . his pendant lips [are] streaming with bloody slaver." "Look . . . how her foot bleeds," Edgar Linton exclaims, and "She may be lamed for life," his mother anxiously notes (chap. 6). Obviously such bleeding has sexual connotations, especially when it occurs in a pubescent girl. Crippling injuries to the feet are equally resonant, moreover, almost always signifying symbolic castration, as in the stories of Oedipus, Achilles, and the Fisher King. Additionally, it hardly needs to be noted that Skulker's equipment for aggression—his huge purple tongue and pendant lips, for instance—sounds extraordinarily phallic. In a Freudian sense, then, the imagery of this brief but violent episode hints that Catherine has been simultaneously catapulted into adult female sexuality *and* castrated.

How can a girl "become a woman" and be castrated (that is, desexed) at the same time? Considering how Freudian its iconographic assumptions are, the question is disingenuous, for not only in Freud's terms but in feminist terms, as Elizabeth Janeway and Juliet Mitchell have both observed, femaleness—implying "penis envy"—quite reasonably *means* castration. "No woman has been deprived of a penis; she never had one to begin with," Janeway notes commenting on Freud's crucial "Female Sexuality" (1931).

> But she *has* been deprived of something else that men enjoy:
> namely, autonomy, freedom, and the power to control her des-
> tiny. By insisting, falsely, on female deprivation of the male
> organ, Freud is pointing to an actual deprivation and one of
> which he was clearly aware. In Freud's time the advantages
> enjoyed by the male sex over the inferior female were, of course,
> even greater than at present, and they were also accepted to a
> much larger extent, as being inevitable, inescapable. Women
> were evident *social* castrates, and the mutilation of their poten-
> tiality as achieving human creatures was quite analogous to the
> physical wound.

But if such things were true in Freud's time, they were even truer in Emily Brontë's. And certainly the hypothesis that Catherine Earnshaw has become in some sense a "social castrate," that she has been "lamed for life," is borne out by her treatment at Thrushcross Grange—and by the treatment of her alter ego, Heathcliff. For, assuming that she is a "young lady," the entire Linton household cossets the wounded (but still healthy) girl as if she were truly an invalid. Indeed, feeding her their alien rich food—negus and cakes from their own table—washing her feet, combing her hair, dressing her in "enormous slippers," and wheeling her about like a doll, they seem to be enacting some sinister ritual of initiation, the sort of ritual that has traditionally weakened mythic heroines from Persephone to Snow White. And because he is "a little Lascar, or an American or Spanish castaway," the Lintons banish Heathcliff from their parlor, thereby separating Catherine from the lover/brother whom she herself defines as her strongest and most necessary "self." For five weeks now, she will be at the mercy of the Grange's heavenly gentility.

To say that Thrushcross Grange is genteel or cultured and that it therefore seems "heavenly" is to say, of course, that it is the opposite of Wuthering Heights. And certainly at every point the two houses are opposed to each other, as if each in its self-assertion must absolutely deny the other's being. Like Milton and Blake, Emily Brontë thought in polarities. Thus, where Wuthering Heights is essentially a great parlorless room built around a huge central hearth, a furnace of dark energy like the fire of Los, Thrushcross Grange has a parlor notable not for heat but for light, for "a pure white ceiling bordered by gold" with "a shower of glass-drops" in the center that seems to parody the "sovran vital Lamp" (*Paradise Lost* 3.22) which illuminates Milton's heaven of Right Reason. Where Wuthering Heights, moreover, is close to being naked or "raw" in Lévi-Strauss' sense—its floors uncarpeted, most of its inhabitants barely literate, even the meat on its shelves open to inspection—Thrushcross Grange is clothed and "cooked": carpeted in crimson, bookish, feeding on cakes and tea and negus. It follows from this, then, that where Wuthering Heights is functional, even its dogs working sheepdogs or hunters, Thrushcross Grange (though guarded by bulldogs) appears to be decorative or aesthetic, the home of lapdogs as well as ladies. And finally, therefore, Wuthering Heights in its stripped functional rawness is essentially anti-hierarchical and egalitarian as the aspirations of Eve and Satan, while Thrushcross Grange reproduces the hierarchical chain of being that Western culture traditionally proposes as heaven's decree.

For all these reasons, Catherine Earnshaw, together with her whip Heathcliff, has at Wuthering Heights what Emily Dickinson would call a "Barefoot-Rank." But at Thrushcross Grange, clad first in enormous, crippling slippers and later in "a long cloth habit which she [is] obliged to hold up with both hands" (chap. 7) in order to walk, she seems on the verge of becoming, again in Dickinson's words, a "Lady [who] dare not lift her Veil / For fear it be dispelled." For in comparison to Wuthering Heights, Thrushcross Grange is, finally, the home of concealment and doubleness, a place where, as we shall see, reflections are separated from their owners like souls from bodies, so that the lady in anxiety "peers beyond her mesh— / And wishes—and denies— / Lest Interview—annul a want / That Image—satisfies." And it is here, therefore, at heaven's mercy, that Catherine Earnshaw learns "to adopt a double character without exactly intending to deceive anyone" (chap. 8).

In fact, for Catherine Earnshaw, Thrushcross Grange in those five fatal weeks becomes a Palace of Instruction, as Brontë ironically called the equivocal schools of life where her adolescent Gondals were often incarcerated. But rather than learning, like A. G. A. and her cohorts, to rule a powerful nation, Catherine must learn to rule herself, or so the Lintons and her brother decree. She must learn to repress her own impulses, must girdle her own energies with the iron stays of "reason." Having fallen into the decorous "heaven" of femaleness, Catherine must become a lady. And just as her entrance into the world of Thrushcross Grange was forced and violent, so this process by which she is obligated to accommodate herself to that world is violent and painful, an unsentimental education recorded by a practiced, almost sadistically accurate observer. For the young Gondals, too, had had a difficult time of it in their Palace of Instruction: far from being wonderful Golden Rule days, their school days were spent mostly in dungeons and torture cells, where their elders starved them into submission or self-knowledge.

That education for Emily Brontë is almost always fearful, even agonizing, may reflect the Brontës' own traumatic experiences at the Clergy Daughters School and elsewhere. But it may also reflect in a more general way the repressiveness with which the nineteenth century educated all its young ladies, strapping them to backboards and forcing them to work for hours at didactic samplers until the more high-spirited girls—the Catherine Earnshaws and Catherine Morlands—must have felt, like the inhabitants of Kafka's penal colony, that the morals and maxims of patriarchy were being embroidered on their own skins. To mention Catherine Morland here is not to digress. As we have seen, Austen did not subject her heroine to education as a Gothic/Gondalian torture, except parodically. Yet even Austen's parody suggests that for a girl like Catherine Morland the school of life inevitably inspires an almost instinctive fear, just as it would for A. G. A. "Heavenly" Northanger Abbey may somehow conceal a prison cell, Catherine suspects, and she develops this notion by sensing (as Henry Tilney cannot) that the female romances she is reading are in some sense the disguised histories of her own life.

In Catherine Earnshaw's case, these points are made even more subtly than in the Gondal poems or in *Northanger Abbey,* for Catherine's education in doubleness, in ladylike decorum meaning also ladylike deceit, is marked by an actual doubling or fragmentation of her personality. Thus though it is ostensibly Catherine who is being educated, it is Heathcliff—her rebellious alter ego, her whip, her id—who is exiled to a prison cell, as if to implement delicate Isabella Linton's first horrified reaction to him: "Frightful thing! Put him in the cellar" (chap. 6). Not in the cellar but in the garret, Heathcliff is locked up and, significantly, starved, while Catherine, daintily "cutting up the wing of a goose," practices table manners below. Even more significantly, however, she too is finally unable to eat her dinner and retreats under the table cloth to weep for her imprisoned playmate. To Catherine, Heathcliff is "more myself than I am," as she later famously tells Nelly, and so his literal starvation is symbolic of her more terrible because more dangerous spiritual starvation, just as her literal wound at Thrushcross Grange is also a metaphorical deathblow to *his* health and power. For divided from each other, the once androgynous Heathcliff-and-Catherine are now conquered by the concerted forces of patriarchy, the Lintons of Thrushcross Grange acting together with Hindley and Frances, their emissaries at the Heights.

It is, appropriately enough, during this period, that Frances gives birth to Hareton, the new patriarch-to-be, and dies, having fulfilled her painful function in the book and in the world. During this period, too, Catherine's education in ladylike self-denial causes her dutifully to deny her self and decide to marry Edgar. For when she says of Heathcliff that "he's more myself than I am," she means that as her exiled self the nameless "gipsy" really does preserve in his body more of her original being than she retains: even in his deprivation he seems whole and sure, while she is now entirely absorbed in the ladylike wishing and denying Dickinson's poem describes. Thus, too, it is during this period of loss and transition that Catherine obsessively inscribes on her windowsill the crucial writing Lockwood finds, writing which announces from the first Emily Brontë's central concern with identity: "a name repeated in all kinds of characters, large and small— Catherine Earnshaw, here and there varied to Catherine Heathcliff, and then again to Catherine Linton" (chap. 3). In the light of this repeated and varied name it is no wonder, finally, that Catherine knows Heathcliff is "more myself than I am," for he has only a single name, while she has so many that she may be said in a sense to have none. Just as triumphant self-discovery is the ultimate goal of the male *bildungsroman,* anxious self-denial, Brontë suggests, is the ultimate product of a female education. What Catherine, or any girl, must learn is that she does not know her own name, and therefore cannot know either who she is or whom she is destined to be.

It has often been argued that Catherine's anxiety and uncertainty about her own identity represents a moral failing, a fatal flaw in her character which leads to her inability to choose between Edgar and Heathcliff. Heathcliff's reproachful "Why did you betray your own heart, Cathy?" (chap. 15) represents a Blakean form of this moral criticism, a contemptuous suggestion that "those who restrain desire do so because theirs is weak enough to be restrained." The more vulgar and commonsensical attack of the Leavisites, on the other hand—the censorious notion that "maturity" means being strong enough to choose not to have your cake and eat it too—represents what Mark Kinkead-Weeks calls "the view from the Grange." To talk of morality in connection with Catherine's fall—and specifically in connection with her self-deceptive decision to marry Edgar— seems pointless, however, for morality only becomes a relevant term where there are meaningful choices.

As we have seen, Catherine has no meaningful choices. Driven from

Wuthering Heights to Thrushcross Grange by her brother's marriage, seized by Thrushcross Grange and held fast in the jaws of reason, education, decorum, she cannot do otherwise than as she does, must marry Edgar because there is no one else for her to marry and a lady must marry. Indeed, her self-justifying description of her love for Edgar—"I love the ground under his feet, and the air over his head, and everything he touches, and every word he says" (chap. 9)—is a bitter parody of a genteel romantic declaration which shows how effective her education has been in indoctrinating her with the literary romanticism deemed suitable for young ladies, the swooning "femininity" that identifies all energies with the charisma of fathers/lovers/husbands. Her concomitant explanation that it would "degrade" her to marry Heathcliff is an equally inevitable product of her education, for her fall into ladyhood has been accompanied by Heathcliff's reduction to an equivalent position of female powerlessness, and Catherine has learned, correctly, that if it is degrading to be a woman it is even more degrading to be *like* a woman. Just as Milton's Eve, therefore, being already fallen, had no meaningful choice despite Milton's best efforts to prove otherwise, so Catherine has no real choice. Given the patriarchal nature of culture, women must fall—that is, they are already fallen because doomed to fall.

In the shadow of this point, however, moral censorship is merely redundant, a sort of interrogative restatement of the novel's central fact. Heathcliff's Blakean reproach is equally superfluous, except insofar as it is not moral but etiological, a question one part of Catherine asks another, like her later passionate "Why am I so changed?" For as Catherine herself perceives, social and biological forces have fiercely combined against her. God as—in W. H. Auden's words—a "Victorian papa" has hurled her from the equivocal natural paradise she calls "heaven" and He calls "hell" into His idea of "heaven" where she will break her heart with weeping to come back to the Heights. Her speculative, tentative "mad" speech to Nelly captures, finally, both the urgency and the inexorability of her fall. "Supposing at twelve years old, I had been wrenched from the Heights . . . and my all in all, as Heathcliff was at that time, and been converted at a stroke into Mrs. Linton, the lady of Thrushcross Grange, and the wife of a stranger: an exile, and outcast, thenceforth, from what had been my world." In terms of the psychodramatic action of *Wuthering Heights,* only Catherine's use of the word *supposing* is here a rhetorical strategy; the rest of her speech is absolutely accurate, and places her subsequent actions beyond good and evil, just as it suggests, in yet another Blakean reversal of customary terms, that her madness may really be sanity.

Wuthering Heights:
At the Threshold of Interpretation

Carol Jacobs

> *"Curiouser and curiouser!" cried Alice (she was so much surprised, that for the moment she quite forgot how to speak good English).*
> —*Alice's Adventures in Wonderland*

Is it Carroll who will articulate for us the dilemma of finding one's way into a literary text? And if Carroll's articulation becomes "curiouser and curiouser" and threatens the possibility of "good English," of the good text, couldn't we nevertheless regard it as a most appropriate entrance into the realm of *Wuthering Heights?* The breakdown in linguistic control announced in the epigraph takes place in the midst of a series of events which are key to the understanding of *Alice's Adventures in Wonderland.* Alice, you will remember, has just fallen down the interminably long rabbit hole only to discover a lengthy hall of locked doors. A tiny gold key fits none of the normal-sized portals but does allow her to open a very small door leading to a wondrous if dangerous garden. Alice may enter this land only at the price of a radical change in her own size, a change proving to be disastrous to the integrity of her self. For at this point follows a shrinking which " 'might end, you know,' said Alice to herself, 'in my going out altogether, like a candle.' " The shrinking is followed by an equally problematical growing which first imposes a bizarre self-estrangement and finally leads Alice to completely doubt the identity of her own voice.

Like the entrance to Wonderland, the entrance to *Wuthering Heights* is marked by the metaphor of the doorway. Passage through that threshold will generate a crisis both in the voice of the self and in the logic of the

From *boundary 2* 7, no. 3 (Spring 1979). © 1979 by *boundary 2.*

good text. As in Carroll's text, where the adventures in Wonderland ultimately fall under the aegis of the dream, so in *Wuthering Heights* one dreams of finding its center only to find that the center is a dream.

We enter *Wuthering Heights* through the voice of Lockwood, who devotes the first three chapters of his narrative to what he twice calls the "repetition of my intrusion." These intrusions are, to be sure, the literal incursions he makes into the house of Wuthering Heights but they function no less as attempts to penetrate *Wuthering Heights*-as-text. The outsider, conventional in language as well as understanding, makes repeated efforts to force his way to the penetralium. Yet one knocks vainly for admittance at these locked doors and, on his second visit, the intruder enters only by means of a violence which almost matches that of Wuthering Heights itself. He penetrates to the innermost chamber of the structure and to the enclosed oaken bed within, and here he experiences the very center of Wuthering Heights as a dream, or, more accurately, as a series of nightmares. This dream-troubled night rapidly results in Lockwood's excommunication from Wuthering Heights, for the illness brought on by these events confines him to Thrushcross Grange. At the same juncture, Nelly Dean replaces Lockwood in his role as narrator, for Lockwood becomes the mere recorder of Nelly's story.

How are we to interpret this curious point of articulation between the first three chapters of the novel and the narrative that follows? Certainly not by taking Lockwood at his word. He organizes his explanation by supressing all further mention of the dreams and by linking the subsequent events into a simplistic causal chain. A sleepless night and a difficult journey through the snow bring on a bad cold. The illness, in turn, incapacitates him, and so he calls in the housekeeper to entertain him with her tales. A fiction surely, for if we return to chapter 3, we find that the texts of the dream dislocate the possibility of such explanation. The exclusion of Lockwood from the Heights and the displacement of Lockwood as direct narrator of the novel, his excommunication from Wuthering Heights both as a banishment from its community and as a relegation to a position outside of communication, are already the common, if oblique, themes of the dreams themselves. They mark the disjunction not only between Lockwood and Wuthering Heights but also between Lockwood and *Wuthering Heights*-as-text. For these passages offer a commentary on the nature of the fictional space marked off as Nelly's narrative, a commentary which is made possible by setting off Lockwood as that which lies outside the fictional realm. The exact locus of this commentary will remain equivocal; for it lies somewhere between Lockwood's puzzlement and Nelly's explanation, and yet again at the heart of *Wuthering Heights*.

Finally closeted within the panelled bed, Lockwood imagines he had delineated a protective boundary between himself and the threatening realm without: "I slid back the panelled sides, got in with my light, pulled them together again, and felt secure against the vigilance of Heathcliff, and every one else." The diary records but two descriptive details of this apparently secure inner space: "a few mildewed books" lie piled in the corner of the window ledge, and the ledge itself is "covered with writing scratched on the paint." Having reached the very center of Wuthering Heights, Lockwood finds it inhabited by texts. And not just any texts. For the scratchings of Catherine and the books of her library, whose margins also contain her diary, figure most significantly in Lockwood's dreams. Each dream incorporates one of these three texts. In the first appear the spectre-like letters etched on the sill. The second concerns the pious discourse of Jabes Branderham, which Lockwood had just begun reading. The third personifies the child Cathy, who speaks from the pages of her diary.

Lockwood's narrative elaborates a system of "careful causality" to establish the relationship between text and dream. He describes himself reading Catherine's name and then dreaming of it. He wakes to find his candle burning one of the good books, and so peruses them. He dreams once again of the text he has just been reading and is awakened by "a shower of load taps on the boards of the pulpit, which responded so smartly that, at last, to my unspeakable relief, they woke me." He locates the dream-source in the title of Jabes's sermon, and its noisy conclusion is easily explained away by assigning it to a referent in the "real world," the branch of the fir tree: "And what was it that had suggested the tremendous tumult, what had played Jabes's part in the row? Merely the branch of a fir tree that touched my lattice, as the blast wailed by, and rattled its dry cones against the panes!" Lockwood attributes his last dream to the reading of Cathy's diary: " 'The truth is, sir, I passed the first part of the night in—' here, I stopped afresh — I was about to say 'perusing those old volumes;' then it would have revealed my knowledge of their written, as well as their printed contents."

Lockwood interprets his dreams by rooting them firmly in his waking world. In this manner he attempts to establish the ascendancy of reality over dream and to dispense with a merely fictional terror by rational explication. Yet the terror of fiction is otherwise. The "reality" by means of which Lockwood claims deliverance is, after all, rather a series of texts. And looking to the dreams themselves, we find they give those texts quite another interpretation. In each of the dreams, the dreamer is engaged in a violent struggle and it is precisely those apparently innocuous texts which function as his vicious adversaries.

The waking Lockwood imagines himself victorious in these conflicts, but the dreams themselves tell the story of a different mastery. First, the glaring letters of Catherine's name swarm at Lockwood; then it is quite literally the text of Jabes Branderham's sermon which assaults him; and, finally, he struggles unsuccessfully with a figure arisen from Cathy's diary, or "an impression which personified itself" out of the name Catherine Linton.

In his second dream, Lockwood is condemned to endure the endless sermon of Jabes Branderham. With each division of the sermon, Lockwood rises to go, but is forced each time to resume his seat:

> Oh, how weary I grew. How I writhed, and yawned, and nodded, and revived! How I pinched and pricked myself, and rubbed my eyes, and stood up, and sat down again, and nudged Joseph to inform me if he would *ever* have done!
> I was condemned to hear all out.

The forgiveness demanded of Lockwood strangely figures as forgiveness of the discourse itself rather than of the sins the text names. The length of the text and especially the repetitive nature of its structure make its textuality more prevalent than its content:

> "Sir," I exclaimed, "sitting here, within these four walls, at one stretch, I have endured and forgiven the four hundred and ninety heads of your discourse. Seventy times seven times have I plucked up my hat and been about to depart—Seventy times seven times have you preposterously forced me to resume my seat. The four hundred and ninety-first is too much."

The four hundred and ninety-first attempt to deny the text, this time by destroying Jabes Branderham, the refusal to forgive the four hundred and ninety-first head of the discourse is the sin for which Lockwood cannot be forgiven. As anticipated, the sentence of excommunication is handed down:

> "*Thou art the Man!*" cried Jabes, after a solemn pause, leaning over his cushion. "Seventy times seven times didst thou gapingly contort they visage—seventy times seven did I take counsel with my soul—Lo, this is human weakness; this also may be absolved! The First of the Seventy-First is come. Brethren, execute upon him the judgment written! such honour have all His saints!"
> With that concluding word, the whole assembly, exalting their pilgrim's staves, rushed round me in a body.

Although its violence is initially masked, it is ultimately the endless text which wields the power to destroy Lockwood.

Lockwood's last dream displays a similar pattern. Here too he must struggle with a textual emanation, a figure from the diary passage just read. The child-spectre clasps his hand, and Lockwood attempts to disengage himself by pulling the child's wrist along the broken window pane. Finally be beguiles her into letting go, and yet, as in his other dreams, his struggle is never definitively won. Neither the piling of the books before him as a barrier nor the stopping of his ears can rid him of the terrifying child's voice.

The waking, rational Lockwood thinks to master this violence by reestablishing the reality of certain texts, but his nightmares mock him. They mimic the structure of his relationship to those same texts and reverse the apparent order of ascendancy.

Lockwood dreams of the texts that lie at the center of Wuthering Heights and in this manner confronts the text of *Wuthering Heights,* the actual narrative begun in chapter 4. Or is it quite the reverse? Perhaps, after all, it is *Wuthering Heights* that dreams here, dreaming of a violent struggle with its other, Lockwood, in order to define a space for its own fiction. Whatever the pattern of confrontation, chapter 3 (its dreams, its texts, its description of Lockwood's coming and going) anticipates all that takes place in the pages that follow. And yet it does not merely anticipate what takes place there *as event.* If chapter 3 is a prefiguration of the narrative to come, it operates as that which literally comes before the figure. It is the image of the figure: *avant la lettre,* it transforms what might otherwise seem to be simple narrative content into the fiction's continual commentary on its own figuration. If the fundamental questions of chapter 3, those of naming, usurpation, homelessness, and passion prove to also hold sway in Nelly's tale of *Wuthering Heights,* they do so as questions previously inscribed as the text's mode of elaborating on its own textuality.

No one has written more suggestively on this relationship between dream and narrative than Frank Kermode. In his recent, very provocative essay "A Modern Way with the Classic," Kermode uses the multiple inscriptions of Catherine's names to elegantly account for the movement of events in the novel.

> When you have processed all the information you have been waiting for, you see the point of the order of the scribbled names, as Lockwood gives them: *Catherine Earnshaw, Catherine Heathcliff, Catherine Linton.* Read from left to right they recapitulate

Catherine Earnshaw's story; read from right to left, the story
of her daughter, Catherine Linton. The names *Catherine* and
Earnshaw begin and end the narrative. . . . this is an account of
the movement of the book: away from Earnshaw and back, like
the movement of the house itself.

To be sure, it is the permutation of names in *Wuthering Heights* which
generates the movement of the text. But is that generation really quite as
ordered as Kermode would have us believe? He openly ascribes the linear
ordering of the names to Lockwood: "you see the point of the order of the
scribbled names, *as Lockwood gives them*" (italics mine) from Catherine
Earnshaw, to Heathcliff, to Linton. And yet, those same names, as they
appear first on the window ledge and then in the dream, elude the reification
that Lockwood imposes. On the window ledge they are simply varied here
and there from one name to the next: "This writing, however, was nothing
but a name repeated in all kinds of characters, large and small—*Catherine
Earnshaw,* here and there varied to *Catherine Heathcliff,* and then again to
Catherine Linton." In the nightmare as well, the names swarm at Lockwood
in no apparent order.

Kermode's interpretation, as radical as it often seems, operates in
strange complicity with Lockwood. We have already seen the fundamental
disparity between the texts and dreams at the center of Wuthering Heights
on the one hand, and Lockwood's account of them on the other. Kermode
here chooses Lockwood's version—and he has his own good reason. Such
a version allows him a linear reading not only of the novel's plot "from
left to right," from beginning to end, but also of the interpretative experience from the " 'hermeneutic' promise" of an early inscription to the
fulfillment of that promise. His reading functions as a processing of information from an indeterminacy of meaning to "the repair of indeterminancy"
and "to the generation of meaning."

The linear reading of events gives the sense of a closed, happy ending,
for Kermode speaks of the "restoration" of true names and of "inheritance
restored" which bring about the emergence of "a more rational culture."
This restoration operates, of course, as a metaphor for Kermode's own
hermeneutic enterprise, for the solution of the dream-rebus given above
appears precisely in terms of restoring names rationally to their proper
place. But Kermode's gesture is double. If with one hand he seems to close
the text of *Wuthering Heights,* with the other he opens it up to "the coexistence . . . of a plurality of significances." With the largesse of liberalism,
he claims "to be reading a text that might well signify differently to different
generations and different persons within those generations."

And yet, *Wuthering Heights* tolerates neither the one gesture nor the other. If we look to the actual functioning of names and the pattern of inheritance within the text, they promise neither a restored rationality nor the comfortably coexistence of equally valid forces. Rather than "signifying differently to different generations," they generate differences.

The uncanny dearth of names may permit linear trajectories for each of the Catherines, but it also fabricates interrelations between other characters which are hardly reducible to linearity. Others too change and gain their identities through the combinatory dance of names in which all major characters take part. The assumption of another's name functions less to advance the plot line than to elaborate complex patterns of differentiation which govern the entire text. Thus the second Catherine Linton can take her mother's name only at the price of distinction:

> It was named Catherine, but he [Edgar] never called it the name in full, as he had never called the first Catherine short, probably because Heathcliff had a habit of doing so. The little one was always Cathy; it formed to him a distinction from the mother, and yet, a connection with her.

> She was the most winning thing that ever brought sunshine into a desolate house—a real beauty in face, with the Earnshaws' handsome dark eyes, but the Lintons' fair skin, and small features, and yellow curling hair. Her spirit was high, though not rough, and qualified by a heart sensitive and lively to excess in its affections. That capacity for intense attachments reminded me of her mother; still she did not resemble her.

If the text plays upon the imperfect repetition of names, it plays no less on the imperfect repetition of personality and feature, for just as Cathy fails to resemble her mother, so Linton Heathcliff only partially resembles his uncle. Nelly describes him as a "pale, delicate, effeminate boy, who might have been taken for my master's younger brother, so strong was the resemblance; but there was a sickly peevishness in his aspect that Edgar Linton never had."

The paradox in this realm of dislocated indentities is that characters nevertheless relate to one another as images of those they only half resemble. Edgar Linton's attachment to his daughter "sprang from its relation to" her mother. Isabella and Linton are metaphors in Heathcliff's eye for Edgar Linton, and Hareton for his own youth: "Five minutes ago, Hareton seemed a personification of my youth, not a human being. I felt to him in such a variety of ways, that it would have been impossible to have accosted him rationally." Everything in Heathcliff's final world swarms as endless signs for Cathy:

> For what is not connected with her to me? and what does not recall her? I cannot look down to this floor, but her features are shaped on the flags! In every cloud, in every tree—filling the air at night, and caught by glimpses in every object by day, I am surrounded with her image! The most ordinary faces of men and women—my own features—mock me with a resemblance. The entire world is a dreadful collection of memoranda that she did exist, and that I have lost her!

In a realm in which all has become pure image, here then is the function of names. Throughout *Wuthering Heights* they resemble that to which they refer, only to mark its absence. Surely this betokens insanity rather than Kermode's promise of rationality restored. But what of Kermode's other alternative, that of a multitude of equally valid significances? This also is ruled out, for the names as we have seen it to function, despotically eliminates its referent, leaving room neither for plurality nor for significance.

It is this same function of names that the pattern of inheritance repeatedly traces. For inheritance in *Wuthering Heights* takes place as a series of usurpations. The family name, once inextricably bound to its property (that of Earnshaw to Wuthering Heights and Linton to Thrushcross Grange), can no longer guarantee possession. On the contrary, the earliest episode of Nelly's tale, the arrival of the parentless, originless child, threatens disjunction between name and property. Heathcliff, never granted the family name, named rather for that which does not exist, a dead child, enters speaking an incomprehensible "gibberish" to dislocate name from referent. This agency of usurpation governs the text, then, from the very beginning.

On what is this relentless will to usurpation based? It figures less as desire for possession than as a bizarre desire for imitation. The object of imitation would seem to be the previous master in the chain of usurpations. Heathcliff, for example, assumes Hindley's place by misusing Hareton almost precisely as Hindley had misused Heathcliff:

> I can sympathize with all his feelings, having felt them myself. I know what he suffers now, for instance, exactly—it is merely a beginning of what he shall suffer, though. And he'll never be able to emerge from his bathos of coarseness and ignorance. I've got him faster than his scoundrel of a father secured me.

And yet, because it is the unwillingness to forgive past infractions which motivates these usurpations, they operate less as imitations of a person than of the gesture of violation, less as the attempt to replace a fixed identity than as the repetition of displacement. As Isabella finally flees Wuthering Heights, she articulates this in terms of demanding an eye for an eye and a tooth for a tooth:

> "But what misery laid on Heathcliff could content me, unless I have a hand in it? I'd rather he suffered it, if I might cause his sufferings and he might *know* that I was the cause. Oh, I owe him so much. On only one condition can I hope to forgive him. It is, if I may take an eye for an eye, a tooth for a tooth; for every wrench of agony, return a wrench, reduce him to my level."

There is hardly a major character who eludes the violence of this displacement. First, Hindley is forced from home. After old Earnshaw's death, Heathcliff is in turn driven away, returning some years later to repeat the dispossession of Hindley. On his death, Heathcliff is replaced by Hareton, who had been left virtually homeless on Heathcliff's return. Isabella's marriage wrenches her from home and leaves her bemoaning the impossibility of return. Even after her escape from Heathcliff, she is forced to live out her life away from Thrushcross Grange. Her son Linton Heathcliff is uprooted first to his uncle's home and then to his father's. The second Catherine is first taken from Thrushcross Grange as Heathcliff's temporary prisoner, and soon becomes his permanent one.

The utlimate figure of homelessness is, of course, the first Cathy, for it is she who creates her exile as a conscious act of the imagination:

> "If I were in heaven, Nelly, I should be extremely miserable. . . . I dreamt, once, that I was there. . . . Heaven did not seem to be my home; and I broke my heart with weeping to come back to earth; and the angels were so angry that they flung me out, into the middle of the heath on the top of Wuthering Heights; where I woke sobbing for joy. That will do to explain my secret, as well as the other. I've no more business to marry Edgar Linton than I have to be in heaven.

The marriage to Edgar fulfills this prophecy of homelessness from which only death promises a respite. Yet Cathy's death, in turn, is yet another self-imposed exile. Lockwood encounters her as the ghostly child-waif who has been wandering for twenty years:

"Let me in—let me in!"

"Who are you?" I asked, struggling, meanwhile, to disengage myself.

"Catherine Linton," it replied, shiveringly (why did I think of *Linton?* I had read *Earnshaw* twenty times for Linton). "I'm come home, I'd lost my way on the moor!" . . .

"It's twenty years," mourned the voice, "twenty years, I've been a waif for twenty years!"

The text casts us back here to Lockwood's dreams, where it is no coincidence that the ultimate figure of homelessness should first have appeared. The entire episode of Lockwood's visit is an allegory of homelessness and excommunication, an allegory which reads and is read by the narrative that follows. As soon as he enters Wuthering Heights, Lockwood senses his exile. The return home is impossible without a guide, and Wuthering Heights, of course, can offer him none:

"I wonder you should select the thick of a snow-storm to ramble about it. Do you know that you run a risk of being lost in the marshes? People familiar with these moors often miss their road on such evenings. . . ."

"Perhaps I can get a guide among your lads, and he might stay at the Grange till morning—could you spare me one?"

"No, I could not."

Because no guide is willingly offered, the intruder desperately rushes for the nearest gate, snatching a lantern to light the dark path back from Wuthering Heights. But this attempt also fails, for Lockwood is attacked by "monsters" who extinguish this last hope for rational illumination: "On opening the little door, two hairy monsters flew at my throat, bearing me down and extinguishing the light."

Lockwood is then forced even deeper into darkness as he enters the inner chamber of the house. He imagines he has located a haven in what proves to be the very center of dislocation. Lockwood dreams of, and on waking experiences, excommunication. This, at least, is the tale of the second nightmare. Lockwood dreams that in Joseph he has found a guide who will finally lead him from Wuthering Heights, but soon he discovers that the path they are taking will not bring him home:

I thought it was morning, and I had set out on my way home, with Joseph for a guide. The snow lay yards deep in our road; and, as we floundered on, my companion wearied me with constant reproaches that I had not brought a pilgrim's staff, telling me I could never get into the house without one. . . .

For a moment I considered it absurd that I should need such a weapon to gain admittance into my own residence. Then, a new idea flashed across me. I was not going there.

(Lockwood and Joseph journey instead to hear a text, the sermon of the famous Jabes Branderham. It is a text whose interpretation we must temporarily defer, but which will offer the novel's most elaborate commentary on the nature of Lockwood's excommunication.)

What they head for is hardly a home, but a chapel:

We came to the chapel. I have passed it really in my walks, twice or thrice. . . . The roof has been kept whole hitherto, but as the clergyman's stipend is only twenty pounds per annum, and a house with two rooms, threatening speedily to determine into one, no clergyman will undertake the duties of the pastor.

It is a crumbling structure in which the crumbling of structure takes place, in which the integrity of the sanctuary is violently destroyed—an appropriate space for the scenario of Lockwood's excommunication.

The dream gives at least one reason for Lockwood's exclusion: "My companion wearied me with constant reproaches that I had not brought a pilgrim's staff, telling me that I could never get into the house without one, and boastfully flourishing a heavy-headed cudgel, which I understood to be so denominated." Lockwood comes without pilgrim staff and cudgel, emblems of wandering on the one hand and estrangement and hostility on the other. It is precisely these roles of wanderer and stranger that Lockwood cannot accept. This is why, although Wuthering Heights continually denies refuge to the wanderer, although its gates offer him "no sympathizing movement," the persistent intruder will nevertheless force his entry repeatedly: "At least, I would not keep my doors barred in the daytime. I don't care—I will get in! So resolved, I grasped the latch and shook it vehemently."

If Lockwood is excommunicated from the Heights, it is also because he refuses to risk relationships which imply fundamental separation; these are, however, the only kind of relationships that Nelly's narrative describes. The novel opens with Lockwood's attempt to construe desolation as a basis for human sympathy. He pretends to have sought out "a situation . . . completely removed from the stir of society," yet on finding Heathcliff a "solitary" man, Lockwood attempts to reconcile the solitary man with the neighbor. "I have just returned from a visit to my landlord—the solitary neighbour that I shall be troubled with. This is certainly a beautiful country! In all England, I do not believe that I could have fixed on a situation so completely removed from the stir of society." The narrator names his new home a "misanthropist's Heaven," and yet misanthropy for Lockwood becomes the ground for communal sharing— "A perfect misanthropist's Heaven—and Mr. Heathcliff and I are such a suitable pair to divide the desolation between us. A capital fellow! He little imagined how my heart warmed towards him when I beheld his black eyes withdraw so suspiciously under their brows." Lockwood repeats with the young Cathy the same mistake he makes with respect to Heathcliff. Here Lockwood elicits no sign of sympathy but nevertheless fantasizes the possibility of marriage.

What is the nature of this fundamental estrangement which *Wuthering Heights* imposes on narrator and characters alike? Surely Lockwood's banal love-fantasies (where desire dreams in vain of coincidence with its object) are but images of something else. The path that finally returns Lockwood to his residence, the space that marks the untraversable distance between Wuthering Heights and home, tells the tale:

> The whole hill-back was one billowy, white ocean, the swells and falls not indicating corresponding rises and depressions in the ground: many pits, at least, were filled to a level; and entire ranges of mounds, the refuse of the quarries, blotted from the chart which my yesterday's walk left pictured in my mind.

The nature of this fundamental estrangement is that between signs and meaning, an impasse of interpretation. For in this remarkable snowscape, there is no correspondence between surface and ground. The risk here is a potential loss of life; but, more significantly it is also the loss which has of necessity already taken place, a loss of reason, of the potential to re-mark, that which the above passage calls a blotting of the chart of the mind. Lockwood continues:

> I had remarked on one side of the road, at intervals of six or seven yards, a line of upright stones, continued through the whole length of the barren: these were erected, and daubed with lime, on purpose to serve as guides in the dark, and also, when a fall, like the present, confounded the deep swamps on either hand with the firmer path: but, excepting a dirty dot pointing up here and there, all traces of their existence had vanished.

The homelessness imposed by *Wuthering Heights* is that of the trace. The trace of existence, and the trace *as existence,* has vanished, for it no longer functions as a substantial sin *of* something, no longer serves as guide, but as a random "dirty dot pointing up here and there" and leading nowhere.

Where, then, are we in *Wuthering Heights?* The theater of naming which governs the text stages a series of tyrannical displacements of the namesake. The pattern of inheritance displays a disjunction of name and property, for property is handed on through usurpation, a gesture which is less that of appropriation than an almost-repetition of the dislocating gesture that preceded it. Little wonder, then, that the problematics of naming and inheritance are paralleled by that of perpetual exile, and that this homelessness figures also as the homelessness of the trace which has lost its powers to identify its referent.

Perhaps this enables us to reread in *Wuthering Heights* that one last refuge of identity, the passion between Catherine and Heathcliff, for this relationship defines itself in terms of those themes of disjunction it would seem to transcend. Passion, as Cathy describes it, is a self-imposed usurpation, willed dispossession of self-unity. Heathcliff is the way in which she names herself: "I *am* Heathcliff." He is an existence of Cathy's beyond herself, in her mind as her own being, and is more Cathy's self than she is. He provides a path of mediation to Cathy's self which at the same time marks the impossibility of coincidence with that self. Passion becomes a mode of self-naming, a self-reflection which is necessarily self-sundering. This is why, when Cathy finally states her love for Heathcliff, she must in the same breath declare her decision not to marry him. Her declaration of love signals their disunion: "It would degrade me to marry Heathcliff now; so he shall never know how I love him."

From the very first mention of this passion (in chapter 3), it appears as separation as well as union, since the passage from Catherine's diary marks the first but definitive break between Heathcliff and herself. The text introduces obliquely or directly all the modes of disjunction already discussed—naming, inheritance, the refusal to forgive, usurpation, wandering, and passion. The passage is written as two separate entries. The first describes a rainy Sunday afternoon at the Heights shortly after the death of Earnshaw—a long sermon by Joseph, the beginning of Cathy and Heathcliff's rebellion by the destruction of good books, the writing of Cathy's diary in the back-kitchen, and a proposed scamper on the moors. Here there is a break in the text. And when Cathy writes again, the crucial first separation between her and Heathcliff has already taken place. The separation she writes of is that imposed by Hindley:

> "My head aches, till I cannot keep it on the pillow; and still I
> can't give over. Poor Heathcliff! Hindley calls him a vagabond,

and won't let him sit with us, nor eat with us any more; and, he says, he and I must not play together, and threatens to turn him out of the house if we break his orders."

The passage is not situated until later in the novel, when it becomes clear that Cathy had written on the first night she and Heathcliff were forced to sleep separately.

The first actual break between the child-lovers occurs at the gap in the diary text—for this gap marks their scamper to Thrushcross Grange, Cathy's first wandering away from Wuthering Heights, her initial encounter with Edgar Linton, and thus the beginning of the split in Cathy herself. That the proposed scamper on the moors takes them to Thrushcross Grange is not stated explicitly in the diary, but a number of details link the rainy Sunday's adventure under the dairy-woman's cloak mentioned by Cathy with that described later in chapter 6. Nelly says that their run on the moors takes place, like that of the diary, on a rainy Sunday following a banishment from the sitting room:

> One Sunday evening, it chanced that they were banished from the sitting room, for making a noise, or a light offence of the kind, and when I went to call them to supper, I could discover them nowhere. . . . The household went to bed; and I, too, anxious to lie down, opened my lattice and put my head out to hearken, though it rained.

And Heathcliff, on returning from Thrushcross Grange, speaks of the same cloak already mentioned in the diary: "Mrs. Linton took off the grey cloak of the dairy maid which we had borrowed for our excursion."

If the text which Lockwood discovers introduces Cathy's passion, it does so only in terms of separation, and it also specifically prefigures the other two gestures of self-exile, death and marriage. The diary entry prefigures her death, because at the height of her fatal illness Cathy longs to return to the bed in which Lockwood had read her text and she recalls the moment described in the second passage of her diary. At the same time, she likens this moment to when she was wrenched from Wuthering Heights on marrying Edgar:

> I thought as I lay there . . . that I was enclosed in the oak-panelled bed at home; and my heart ached with some great grief which, just waking, I could not recollect. . . . I was a child; my father was just buried, and my misery arose from the separation that Hindley had ordered between me and Heathcliff. I was laid

> alone, for the first time, and, rousing . . . I lifted my hand to
> push the panels aside . . . and then memory burst in. . . . I
> cannot say why I felt so wildly wretched . . . for there is scarcely
> cause. But, supposing at twelve years old, I had been wrenched
> from the Heights, and every early association, and my all in all,
> as Heathcliff was at that time, and been converted at a stroke
> into Mrs. Linton.

Cathy's diary first introduces the tale of *Wuthering Heights* that Nelly will go on to narrate. The tale, then, doesn't begin at the beginning but opens by marking the initial break in the only relationship that approaches perfect identity. At the same time it sets up the central pattern of violent severance that organizes the novel. Strange that this diary which stresses disjunction and rebellion should be found within the covers of "good books." Cathy's diary has been penned as an interpretation of the religious books of her library, an interpretation which contributes to their dilapidation:

> Catherine's library was select, and its state of dilapidation proved
> it to have been well used, though not altogether for a legitimate
> purpose; scarcely one chapter had escaped pen and ink com-
> mentary—at least, the appearance of one—covering every mor-
> sel of blank that the printer had left.

Perhaps not so coincidentally, this diary which devours the textual margin also relates the initial step of Cathy's rebellion as the destruction of the good books that Joseph forces her and Heathcliff to read.

> "Saying this, he compelled us so to square our positions that
> we might receive . . . a dull ray to show us the text. . . .
> "I could not bear the employment. I took my dingy volume
> by the scroop, and hurled it into the dog-kennel, vowing I hated
> a good book."

On being banished to the back-kitchen, Cathy continues her rebellion by writing her diary alongside Jabes Branderham's pious discourse, and thus destroying the "good book."

Cathy wished to destroy Jabes's pious writing, yet the text which Cathy comments on, or at least the only version we have of it (that given in Lockwood's dream), rather than being destroyed by the interpretation seems strangely to enter into the spirit of Cathy's world of non-forgiveness and revenge. The text which one expects to preach the turning of the other cheek ultimately demands an eye for an eye and a tooth for a tooth. When

Lockwood finally fails to forgive the text by refusing to listen further, when he accuses the text and demands the annihilation of its source, Branderham accuses Lockwood in return and demands the narrator's annihilation.

Jabes Branderham's sermon, like Cathy's diary, is itself a commentary on a "good book." The discourse, entitled "Seventy Times Seven, and the First of the Seventy-First," interprets a passage from the New Testament. Although Branderham's comments seem at first to violate the text they interpret (for surely, here in the holiest of texts, one expects to find a call to forgiveness), in fact, Matt. 18:21–35 already contains its own deconstruction. In the earlier verses, Jesus apparently preaches unending forgiveness:

> Then came Peter to him, and said, "Lord, how oft shall my brother sin against me, and I forgive him? till seven times?"
>
> Jesus saith unto him, "I say not unto thee, Until seven times: but, Until seventy times seven."

Yet when Jesus relates a parable to illustrate God's limitless capacity for forgiveness, it culminates rather with the refusal to forgive. The lord who represents God in the parable forgives his servant his debt, but only until the servant himself fails to forgive his debtor. When the servant commits this sin (the first of the seventy-first), the lord demands an eye for an eye and a tooth for a tooth:

> Then his lord, after that he had called him, said unto him, "O thou wicked servant, I forgave thee all that debt, because thou desiredst me:
>
> Shouldest not thou also have had compassion on thy fellow-servant, even I had pity on thee?"
>
> And his lord was wroth, and delivered him to the tormentors, till he should pay all that was due unto him.
>
> So likewise shall my heavenly Father do also unto you, if ye from your hearts forgive not every one his brother their trespasses.

The Biblical text pretends to preach unending forgiveness, yet God himself pays back sins in kind. Thus both Cathy's seemingly destructive commentary on Branderham and Branderham's on Matthew are already contained in the good books they interpret.

The complicated relationship between Lockwood's narrative and the tale of *Wuthering Heights* is rather the reverse of these commentary-text relationships. Whereas both Cathy and Branderham comment destructively on apparently pious texts, Lockwood tries to convert a disturbingly menacing tale into a "good book." He wishes to regard Nelly's tale as benign entertainment. Just as he speaks of his dreams as superstition and uncontrolled imagination, he repeatedly hints at the merely fictional and formal nature of the story. He speaks of Heathcliff as the "hero" of the narrative when the actual person stood at his bedside but a short time before. And although he has actually encountered most of the people in the history he hears, he refers to them as literary "characters."

As we have seen, the language of *Wuthering Heights* insists upon irresolvable disjunction, yet for Lockwood Nelly's language functions as the means for uniting people, as a form of sociability:

> I, who had determined to hold myself independent of all social intercourse, and thanked my stars that, at length, I had lighted on a spot where it was next to impracticable . . . was finally compelled to strike my colours; and, under pretence of gaining information concerning the necessities of my establishment, I desired Mrs. Dean . . . to sit down while I ate . . . hoping sincerely she would prove a regular gossip.

Even when Lockwood begins to sense that *Wuthering Heights* is not quite the unambiguous amusement he sought, he continues to convert the ominous into the beneficial: "Dree, and dreary! I reflected . . . and not exactly of the kind which I should have chosen to amuse me. But never mind! I'll extract wholesome medicines from Mrs. Dean's bitter herbs."

Lockwood makes clear this tendency to extract wholesome medicine from bitter herbs when (in chapter 3) he attempts to protect himself from the ghost-child of his last dream by throwing up a barrier of texts. "The fingers relaxed, I snatched mine through the hole, hurriedly piled the books up in a pyramid against it." These are, to be sure, *good* books, and Lockwood expects the good text to exorcise an evil which he perceives as coming from the other side of the window pane—from without. He all but forgets that the terrifying figure of the ghost-child emanates rather from within the margins of those same texts.

Lockwood closes his narration as he began it, by extracting a benevolent resolution from a text which is at best duplicitous. In his last journey from Wuthering Heights to Thrushcross Grange, the narrator makes a diversion in the direction of the kirk, the same path taken in the second of his dreams. Here he seeks out the graves of Edgar, Cathy, and Heathcliff. Despite Nelly's report that Heathcliff and Cathy have been known to *"walk,"* Lockwood chooses to imagine peaceful slumbers for the two lovers: "I lingered round them, under that benign sky; watched the moths fluttering among the heath and hare-bells; listened to the soft wind breathing through the grass; and wondered how any one could ever imagine unquiet slumbers for the sleepers in that quiet earth." Just as he once struggled to free himself from Cathy's ghost and tried to dispel her spectre-like name, so now Lockwood chooses to believe that the menacing supernatural lies at rest. In this manner the "good book" of *Wuthering Heights* concludes, a tale enclosed within the covers of Lockwood's reassuring narrative and therefore mediated by his interpretation.

Yet Lockwood's conclusion ironically echoes an earlier error of an equally mystified narrator—Nelly Dean. On Cathy's death, Nelly convinces herself that Cathy has returned peacefully home to heaven:

> Her brow smooth, her lids closed, her lips wearing the expression of a smile. No angel in heaven could be more beautiful than she appeared. . . . My mind was never in a holier frame than while I gazed on that untroubled image of Divine rest. . . . "Whether still on earth or now in heaven, her spirit is at home with God!"

The pathetic agony of the ghost-child in Lockwood's dream contradicts Nelly's sentimentalism. And Nelly forgets what Cathy herself has said. The stay in heaven would hardly promise "Divine rest," but rather a miserable exile from home. For Cathy either alternative, heaven or earth, is a banishment from home. Although Lockwood and Nelly have both had evidence of Cathy's restless wandering—Lockwood in his dream and Nelly in her observation of Heathcliff's last days—neither seriously acknowledges the possibility that the endless struggle between polarities must yet continue. The union of Hareton and the second Catherine, their move to Thrushcross Grange, leaves Wuthering Heights to their spectre opposites and counterparts, Heathcliff and his Cathy:

> "They are going to the Grange, then?" I said.
> "Yes," answered Mrs. Dean. . . .
> "And who will live here then?"
> "Why, Joseph will take care of the house, and, perhaps, a lad to keep him company. They will live in the kitchen, and the rest will be shut up."
> "For the use of such ghosts as choose to inhabit it," I observed.
> "No, Mr. Lockwood," said Nelly, shaking her head. "I believe the dead are at peace, but it is not right to speak of them with levity."

What is in question here is not only a particular ending to the tale of *Wuthering Heights* but the sense of an ending altogether, which is to say an ending with sense, one that puts to rest all wandering and all generation of contradictory forces. We have already seen Lockwood's determination to fix the boundaries of textuality in his second dream. There, the dreamer was able to forgive exactly seven times seventy heads of Branderham's sermon. The first of the seventy-first is the moment of crisis precisely because, in exceeding the definitive and literal limits set on the discourse, Branderham's text can no longer be controlled. The "ending" that Lockwood imposes on *Wuthering Heights* is a gesture of the same kind.

However benignly Lockwood closes his interpretive narration of *Wuthering Heights,* the text itself always countercomments his conclusions. Within the good book that Lockwood narrates is the story of the fictional nature of his textual posture, an interpretation of its interpreter. Which, then, is the narrator and which the narrated? As the tale begins in chapter 3 and as it ends in chapter 24, Lockwood desperately tries to keep the menacing text under his control. The excommunication which results from his first struggles with the text is also the result of his last attempts to suppress the supernatural by setting limits to the narrative. Lockwood is once again silenced and displaced as narrator. His position is usurped by a text which, because founded on disjunctive self-reading, repeatedly deconstructs itself as "good book." Lockwood's conception of literature is one fiction among many which the novel narrates. It creates this fiction in order to excommunicate it, in order to define itself over and against that which it is not.

Wuthering Heights is an annunciation of excommunication, both a fabrication in language of the real world—of that which is outside language (ex-communication)—and then again an explusion of the heretic from its own textuality. The outsider from that "real world" who enters the closed space of Wuthering Heights is peremptorily banished. Yet this excommunication of Lockwood is not simply an explusion to a position so distant that he no longer threatens what one is tempted to conceive of as the true inside nature of fiction. Excommunication is also incorporation of what the text posits to be its other. Rather than allowing Lockwood to separate himself, it holds him in a relationship to itself of violent difference. It risks itself by allowing Lockwood's conception of fiction its apparent victory.

Wuthering Heights is (about) this struggle between fiction and nonfiction. The fictional space is not a home for fiction, securely bound off from the threats of a world that calls itself real. Fiction is always in exile from itself. It involves the elaboration of and repeated struggle with this other realm, a continual marking of the discrepancy between itself and that which claims to lie outside. At the same time that fiction defines itself as this disjunction, it renounces the possibility of absolute self-definition, not only because it can "define" itself only through its other but also because no delineating boundary can then be drawn—no limits set to the voracious realm of fiction. It is perhaps after all not mere superstition that causes Lockwood to struggle against the dream-texts, for, as the fictional work marks the discrepancy between itself and that which lies outside, it paradoxically threatens to incorporate all that is within its reach, to assimilate the "real" into its own fiction. Lockwood is genuinely at stake in the textuality of the text and this is indicated by the increasingly violent relationship of Lockwood and text in the course of his three dreams. His dreams go through him like wine through water: they write him/his language into their fiction.

The fabrication of Lockwood is the means by which *Wuthering Heights* speaks of its own textuality, and the relationship between Lockwood and the tale of Wuthering Heights is in turn the gap that makes the critical language of this paper possible—a gap that I have generated, perhaps only to close. But what does this alternate generation and closure imply? The implications are critical in several senses. If I have generated the disparity between Lockwood as narrator and the narrative fiction, criticizing throughout Lockwood's naiveté, this judgment necessarily falls prey to the very illusions it pretends to disparage. Although Lockwood's conception of language is a fiction created by the novel, my own text is forced to take Lockwood literally, to pose at least the imaginative possibility of a language that means what it says and refers to a realm outside the insanity of its own self-reflection. Critical rhetoric depends on temporarily forgetting the madness copresent with the "knowledge" that all is language. This forgetfulness gives free play to a referent in my own language, which itself, after all, has pretensions to discursive truth. No less than Lockwood, then, I am at stake in the novel's textuality. In fact, my enterprise has become critical in yet another sense of the word—which brings us to the crisis of interpretation in the question of closure. I have elaborated a commentary whose theoretical stance implicitly insists on remaining within the enclosure of *Wuthering Heights*. How, then does my text fit in? Perhaps, too well. For the supplemental discourse I have offered to add, a deconstruction of Lockwood's narration, was, of necessity, already accounted for. This paper is perhaps yet another fiction that the novel itself has fabricated.

Baby-Work: The Myth of Rebirth in *Wuthering Heights*

Stevie Davies

Catherine Linton, as her mind turns toward its last agony, the departure from the "little frame" in which the warring gods of her spirit contend, moves from violence to a disconcerting lull in which she starts to pull feathers out of her pillow and arrange them methodically on the sheet according to their different species. Her calm absorption in this work of sorting is more frightening than the hysterical fits that preceded it. It is almost as if she had broken through into another world or dimension, abstracted from the chronology of ordinary time, the limits of accepted space, into a quiet place which is inaccessible to anyone else, a sealed solitude. Nelly Dean, who watches and listens, is clearly alarmed and dismayed: she covers her sense of threat by labelling Catherine's occupation "childish," a "childish diversion." She feels that if only Catherine—who is a nuisance—could be got to pull herself together and behave like a normal person, everything could be solved. Nelly's response is the sort that is appropriate and efficient in dealing with a small child's tantrum: you turn your back, avert your eyes and apply an abrasive scepticism. She is right in one sense that Catherine is being "childish," for she has diverted herself entirely. She has gone straight through that invisible wall that separates our adult selves from our childhood selves, as if entering the looking-glass. In the looking-glass world (and Catherine is about to see herself reflected in the mirror which she takes for the old wooden press where she slept in her childhood) perception of time is altered. Childhood is now, immediate.

From *Emily Brontë: The Artist as a Free Woman.* © 1983 by Stevie Davies. Carcanet Press, 1983.

But old age is simultaneous too: Catherine sees Nelly all grey and bent, as she will be, fifty years from this date. Catherine can speak back into the "real" world from the dreamworld, but she communicates as if from far away. All Nelly is definitely aware of is the chaos Catherine is creating in the room as she starts tearing feathers out of the pillow by the handful and scattering them wholesale, blithely unconcerned that Nelly is going to have to pick up the mess and put things to rights. (Nelly as narrator of *Wuthering Heights* is constantly concerned with tidying and putting to rights for Lockwood's and the reader's sake the chaotic material of her story.) She feels cross and surly. " 'Give over that baby-work!' I interrupted." Getting hold of the annoying pillow, she drags it by force out of the plucking hands that are destroying it. All that she—and we—have to compare such an irruption with is the destructive wantonness of childhood in its "baby-work," which is wanton because it does not conceive of consequences. "Baby-work" is an experiment on the wrong side of the boundary between anarchy and survival. Yet the minute we have heard Nelly reduce Catherine's strange activities to this level, we know that she is wrong. We sympathize with Nelly in her task of coping with the feather-spreading, uncontrollable girl on the bed in her delirium: by making us wryly amused at her predicament in the earthy Yorkshire idiom of her reaction to it, Nelly also helps us to cope with it. But we have seen Catherine expressing herself in an activity which cannot accurately be construed as meaninglessly destructive. Beneath the elemental tantrum is taking place a kind of "work" which is mysterious and purposeful. This "baby-work" involves an urge toward a fundamental and radical order, which underlies the common "civilized" order and deeply criticizes it. Beside the work of sorting and grading the feathers in the pillow, social order appears as a kind of primitive chaos.

There is a very ancient story with its roots in Egyptian and Greek mystery religions, of Psyche and a sort of "baby-work" in which she was engaged. Psyche, having lost her lover, Cupid, by exposing him to light, was forced out of her cave into the terrible light of the upper world. The vindictive goddess Venus gave Psyche an impossible task to perform. She was given a huge heap of mixed seeds to sort; a time-limit; and a threat of death in the event of failure. Nobody could do what was required of Psyche: it is not in human nature to fulfil this pointless and immensely detailed task. Psyche was aided by the powers of nature. The end of her story was initiation into full possession of her husband. Psyche is the human spirit— our souls in their first rising to consciousness, losing hold of our primal source and our first intuitive affinities; forcibly separated from our twinned "other self" (Cupid); released into a light which we cannot love, for it exposes us, abandoned and rejected, to a riddling life burdened with tasks whose meaning is lost on us. Life is imagined as a quest, a seeking, shot through with yearning. Yet some potent forces work for us, mysteriously buried in the dark underworld of our nature, where darkness is creative; seeds are growing. The pointless "baby-work" leads, as in all great structuring myths, to rediscovery, reunion and return in a changed form to an earliest truth with which we are finally able to deal.

The legend of Psyche is an allegory of the soul's expulsion, quest, and reunion with the beloved. *Wuthering Heights,* with its story of Catherine's wilful separation from her "twin," Heathcliff, her exile at Thrushcross Grange, the riddle of her delirium and the "baby-work" of her pregnancy and delivery of the new Catherine, is an original myth of loss, exile, rebirth, and return. It has the self-contained and opaque quality of all myth. It imagines the human soul as being female, seeking a lost male counterpart. The "secret" of *Wuthering Heights* is not a displaced incest motif, nor is it asexual, as critics claim. Catherine, having betrayed the union with her own truest likeness, is involved in a sexual search, but sexual union is not the subject of the story, rather it is the metaphor for a search which is metaphysical and "human" in the largest sense. Both Psyche's and Catherine's stories concern a metamorphosis. As the pupa opens to reveal the caterpillar, the caterpillar is bound into the chrysalis, and the chrysalis at its right season is unbound to reveal the new and sticky-winged butterfly which was there at every stage—an eternal and traditional image of rebirth— so Psyche must emerge; her world must darken and bind her; she must toil, despair, change, open, in order to rediscover. But she finds the beloved in her own person. Emily Brontë too stresses the suffering of those metamorphoses, the cramping pain of constriction, the terrible aspects of those rites of passage which initiate one into a new state. Catherine's is not a personal success-story like Psyche's. Emily charts two stages of metamorphosis: dead Catherine gives rite of passage to living Cathy. Like Psyche's the path is full of the most impossible riddles. She cannot trust her eyesight. The agony of death is the same as the agony of birth. It is dreadful to be born; hard to grow up; incomprehensible to die—and Emily Brontë will not say where exactly the new self in her myth of rebirth is located— whether in Heathcliff, in the second Cathy, in the heath where Catherine is buried. Emily preserves the mystery.

All along the way we are presented with images of the most astonishing beauty which, rooted in pain, loss, and dissolution bear suggestions of new life, and the release of the soul from the mortal carcass in which it is borne, as if waiting to hatch and fly. This is most deeply connected with the "baby-work" of which Nelly complains so bitterly. Catherine reacts with ire to the thought of Edgar self-enclosed and adult, composedly reading in his book-lined study, for it is unbearable to her ego to think of him absorbed in the cocoon of his adult preoccupations: " 'What in the name of all that feels, has he to do with *books,* when I am dying?' " She reacts with childish pique to his apparent safety from her tantrums. But at the same time, she responds with a deeper childlikeness of spirit which relates her both to her own orphaned childhood and to the child who is yet to be derived from her, Cathy. The challenge to her power is the catalyst that starts off the "childish diversion" with the pillow, accompanied by a speech that echoes Ophelia's in her madness in Shakespeare's *Hamlet,* but which turns the reader's imagination progressively out of doors—away from books, rooms, the confined space of the present moment, into the immensity of the external world of the heath and of Heathcliff:

> "That's a turkey's," she murmured to herself; "and this is a wild-duck's; and this is a pigeon's. Ah, they put pigeon's feathers in the pillows—no wonder I couldn't die! Let me take care to throw it on the floor when I lie down. And here is a moorcock's; and this—I should know it among a thousand—it's a lapwing's. Bonny bird; wheeling over our heads in the middle of the moor. It wanted to get to its nest, for the clouds touched the swells, and it felt rain coming. This feather was picked up from the heath, the bird was not shot—we saw its nest in the winter, full of little skeletons. Heathcliff set a trap over it, and the old ones dare not come. I made him promise he'd never shoot a lapwing, after that, and he didn't. Yes, here are more! Did he shoot my lapwings, Nelly? Are they red, any of them? Let me look."

All this while, Catherine is removing feathers from her pillow and sorting them. As she sorts them, she names them. As she names them, she relates them to her own destiny. There is a language of flowers, trees, birds, and animals which has still not died out. It is related to that folklore legend for which, given its tough, enduring roots in her inheritance, Emily Brontë had a tenacious memory. Each bird Catherine names springs into life in our imaginations from the bits of feather which are its sole mortal remains, taken by human hands from the carcass of a bird known to us both for its own beauty as a natural creature and for its traditional meaning and suggestions. The domesticated turkey gives way to the wild duck which is an emblem of freedom but hunted by man. Then the Yorkshire superstition that pigeon's feathers restrain the human spirit from passing out of the body is supplied by Catherine as an explanation of why she cannot "burst the fetters" of her condition by willing death so intensely. The pigeon is gregarious, tame, obedient, associated with domesticity and the "homing" instinct that binds her to Thrushcross Grange: she is bound to a continuing and unwanted life in a social order in which she is expected to act the wife's part, that tame, unspirited profession. The moorcock leads out beyond the range of the domestic world in which she is suffocating. Outside all this is the lapwing nesting upon the upland heath, in some shallow exposed basin of the earth, rearing its young at the mercy of every intruder. The lapwing and its baby birds are an exact emblem of Catherine's nature and her plight.

Catherine speaks as if in a waking dream, of a place in which she will never again be a presence; nor is the lapwing at that moment a presence. It is midwinter, and the lapwings have probably migrated. Male lapwings return to choose the site of a breeding-ground in mid-February or March: by that time, when Linton brings her the wild golden crocuses Catherine will be dying. She is within this "shattered prison," her body, enclosed within that other prison of Edgar's house, in extremity, and engaged in the "baby-work" of undoing the stuffing of a pillow, the symbol of all the warmth and comfort that pads and dulls her existence at Thrushcross Grange. Someone has made this pillow, the paranoid's "they"; some enemy to the person she is. She takes what "they" have fabricated to pieces and restructures it; traces the finished (dead) product back to its living sources. Birds have died to make the pillow on which she is meant to lay her head. In the pillow many species' feathers are anarchically mingled: muddle, chaos, is revealed as the basis of the pillow—that, and cruelty too, for much killing of beautiful natural creatures had to be done in order to make up the pillow. Catherine reveals in this most poignant moment that the civilized world, priding itself on its rationality, mildness, and gentle behaviour (Edgar reading in his library) depends on exploitation. She pulls out the inside and analyses it down into its unthinkable reality. Her will is to undo it all: unweave the mess that poses as order and remake the lives on which it preyed. The urge is to return to source. The task, like Psyche's, is not in any way viable unless the riddle can be solved, the code broken, which explains the system in which we all grow. There is a strong sense that this passage is making some emotional and philosophical assault on us with which we are called upon to come to terms. The likelihood is that we respond to the unanswerable by turning with Nelly to the safe haven of a request to "Give over with that baby-work."

But as we move out in imagination on to the heath where the single lapwing swerves and rides the air currents, turning for its nest, we also move back in time, to a single occasion before that great loss of Heathcliff which cut through Catherine's life like a physical bereavement. The piteous image of the nest in the "middle of the moor," seen in winter by the two children "full of little skeletons" is a central symbol within *Wuthering Heights*. We later gather that Catherine, speaking this memory to Nelly, who has decided not to comprehend it, is pregnant. She speaks, in a tradition known in Yorkshire, of the moorland bird as a symbol of the soul liberated from the body, or wandering the earth yearning for heaven. One of Emily Brontë's profoundest affinities is with the wild birds who are almost the sole living inhabitants of the moors. She had observed their habits and behaviour, and studied the natural science of Bewick's *History of British Birds,* painstakingly copying out in minute detail the engravings there. *Wuthering Heights* bears the fruit of this knowledge. Like humankind, the bird-life of the novel speaks of a search for liberty, soaring between the mountains; like our race, their fertility is burdened with seasonal change, the cruelty that is within nature, the high mortality-rate which took such a toll in Emily's own life and which in her art she both expressed realistically and tried to heal in the course of a mythic, cyclical structure. *Wuthering Heights,* in the person of Catherine, tells of a world which is a mighty orphanage, in which at best we are fostered for a limited period, on sufferance. But equally through the person of Catherine, it suggests the process through which we may guess at the existence of kin, seek them out, bond and mate with them, whether on this side of the grave or on the other. And so the birds of Catherine's reverie symbolize her predicament, and suggest its universal nature. The lapwing is near relation of the golden plover whose overhead whistling has, in a northern legend, been associated with the doomed Jews, wandering eternally after the crucifixion; the plaintive curlew's low-pitched fluting was associated in the north with the "Seven Whistlers," portending death. Emily Brontë is able to harness the power of these ancient legends of birds whose inhuman music calls like an agent of destiny into the human world. Yet the creatures Catherine lists are also felt as real, living and warm presences, linked to people not just as messengers but because they are so like us. The lapwing especially is known by its behaviour-patterns as a parent-bird. Its "pee-weet" note extends when its young are in danger to an acutely distressful call, uttered in tumbling flight. The parent-birds feign to be crippled or to drag a wing in order to draw off danger from the exposed nest. The woman who looks back on the outing to the moors where she and Heathcliff were most at home sees an image of beauty—"Bonny bird"; freedom "wheeling over our heads," shot through with menace, inexhaustible longing for home which belongs equally to human and to animal nature, as an instinct rather than a decision. Catherine imagines the bird as having freely moulted the feather she has picked out of her pillow, but the bird was as subject to vicissitude as she now is, pathetic in its longing as she will be in a few minutes, lying back on the much-criticized pillows, "her face bathed in tears . . . our fiery Catherine was no better than a wailing child!" The lapwing is like her in being a parent, with the elements gathering against her: rain is coming. In the midst of its soaring flight it is a prisoner, like Catherine, dashing for home before calamity can strike. Catherine is five months pregnant: she is herself a nest from which the future will derive. Yet her image is of that time after the breeding-season in which (winter then as now) she and Heathcliff were out again and saw the nest "full of little skeletons." This desolating vision of a small family of forms bereaved at their very inception, yet held cocooned in the circle of the nest, their home become a tomb open to the winter skies, is an image for what Catherine feels she holds within her, fertility that is blighted because it comes of Linton. Equally it is an emblem of her own childhood, orphaned like this, exposed in a family of two with Heathcliff after the death of her father and protector, to the enmity and indifference of an uncaring sky.

We always are, in Emily's mythology, the child we were. At the very centre of the novel, in the protracted death of Catherine, the birth of Cathy, this truth is affirmed and reaffirmed. In looking at that nest, barred with a trap, with its starved, exposed little skeletons, we remember that terrible first grief of Catherine as a child:

> The poor thing discovered her loss directly—she screamed out—
> "Oh, he's dead, Heathcliff! he's dead!"
> And they both set up a heart-breaking cry. I joined my wail
> to theirs, loud and bitter.

The only adult present, Joseph, somewhat less than true to the vigorous spirit of the departed, and utterly, satirically unmoved by the grief of the orphans that remain, lets forth a blast of chilling moral air by wanting to know "what we could be thinking of to roar in that way over a saint in Heaven." In their mutual shock and grief, Catherine and Heathcliff become one with the narrator, Nelly: their loss is hers, and the infuriating Catherine with her naughty ways, her petulance and her need, becomes for Nelly "the poor thing." Catherine, after so many times teasing her father till he was moved to say the unthinkable " 'Nay, Cathy . . . I cannot love thee,' " had come on the last evening of his life to lay her head quietly against him; Heathcliff's young head pillowed on her lap; moved to kiss him goodnight, put her arms round his neck and found him dead. Nelly cannot get to the children in their grief. She looks in through their bedroom door late that night and sees that:

> The little souls were comforting each other with better thoughts than I could have hit on; no parson in the world ever pictured Heaven so beautifully as they did, in their innocent talk.

We have been allowed to see a nest of little orphans, cut off for ever from the parent who was their only guarantee of shelter. They are exposed to the rancorous humours of Joseph; the jealousies of Hindley; the intermittent mothering that Nelly can or will give. Our minds touch upon that memory when we read of the dead lapwing chicks in their nest on the moors, cradled in their grave. What Catherine remembers of that vision of the dead young birds carries for us another painful acknowledgment. It was Heathcliff who in his young, unmitigated cruelty, set the trap that introduced the fledglings so early to their mortality. Catherine starts looking for evidence of blood upon the feathers she has pulled from the pillow. Heathcliff, whom she has said she does not love but rather *is*—like a part of her own identity, a force of her own nature—is implicated in the cruelties of the human and the natural world. Later in the novel he will "lay the trap" over the nest of the child Hareton and his own son, Linton Heathcliff, degrading the one and tormenting the other without any hint of remorse. The "little soul" whom Nelly watched with awe in his bereavement communing with Catherine suffers only to cause more suffering. In her poetry, Emily Brontë had constantly reverted to the theme of a rejected child handicapped throughout life because of rough early conditions,

> bred the mate of care,
> The foster-child of sore distress.

Pain begets cruelty; rejection unkindness, reciprocally, so that we act as transmitters down the generations of the wrongs that are done us. It is less a case of original sin than of original pain. That is why Emily Brontë everywhere insists on universal forgiveness for all offences whatever. Seeing through the walls of the adult self to the defenceless child each person contains, it is not thinkable to cast the first stone. Catherine recognizes Heathcliff's "fierce, pitiless, wolfish" nature: " 'he'd crush you, like a sparrow's egg, Isabella.' " He is the barbarous cruelty of the heath itself, with its lowering weather; the wild part of Catherine's own nature which she had thought to have tamed, but also the victim of that pattern with which Emily was so personally familiar, whereby the world is a system for orphaning the young; bringing to destitution; killing mothers; undoing twins; betraying affinities. Heathcliff, who is the agent of so much destruction in *Wuthering Heights,* is as automatically an innocent as any being born into such a system.

At the very centre of the whole novel, Catherine suffers, dies, and gives birth. If we take a radius from that point, we encompass the whole novel, so that the structure is a perfect circle. Like the great myths of antiquity, *Wuthering Heights* presents us not only with a story of rebirth but also with a myth of return. The narrative at once presses forward and doubles back to its source. From the first Hareton Earnshaw who built the Heights in 1500, we are brought to the last Hareton Earnshaw, who restores the ancient line. Though the novel is precisely timed and documented to the year, the day, the hour, almost to a fault, and the very first word is a date (1801), the forward push of heredity and causality, with its vigilant eye on the clock, is retarded by a process of recapitulation. From Catherine's speech about the lapwings, we can move to almost any other point in this great prose poem and find some echo or resonance. Devices such as repetition and recapitulation of places, persons, events, names, and even of the letters which begin those names—the mysterious 'H's of Hindley, Hareton, Heathcliff, suggestive of a family cluster of improbable likenesses, and even a provocative code which tempts us to try and break it—reinforce this sense of a circling reality. Lockwood's narrative encircles Nelly's, which in turn encircles other stories told in their own persons by Zillah, Catherine, Isabella, Heathcliff, in letters, or retold dreams, or simply verbally. The beginning echoes in the end; the end in the beginning. Fractionally before the mathematical centre (so perfectly is the whole novel balanced), the elder Catherine dies and the younger is born; yet the dead Catherine is felt by a reader as just as strong and living a presence in the second half as her daughter and namesake. In the cross-breedings of the two families, the mild Lintons and the harsher Earnshaws, washed through and renewed by fresh blood, there is a sense of something fated and inevitable. The personalities of the characters, though so odd and eccentric, come to seem, in this inexplicable pattern of return to source, as impersonal as their setting, the wind that is busy on the moors and the abeyance of self that is under the moors.

The novel is not so much about individuals as about humanity. It is less about humanity than humanity in a setting. It is far less about humanity in the person of the male of our species ("man," "forefathers," "God the father," "masterpiece") as about humanity in the person of the female. The author of *Genesis,* looking back to our origins, had felt called upon to attribute to Adam a sort of womb where his ribcage was, by biological sleight and to the confounding of common sense, deriving woman from man. For a person as radical as Emily Brontë, and innocent of the offence her perceptions might cause the vulnerable minds of the orthodox, writing of the theme of genesis, this would simply not seem sensible, credible, or even efficient according to the laws of practical economy. She expresses instead a female vision of genesis, expulsion, and rebirth in terms of the metaphor of fertility and childbirth. Wordsworth and the Romantic poets, whom she deeply admired, had taken the imagination back to childhood, to muse over the idea of the child as "father of the man," a metaphor for our beginnings. Emily Brontë, in a way that is radical and difficult because no language has existed in patriarchal England to express it (foremothers, mistress piece, God the mother?), relived the idea according to the more natural metaphor of the child as mother of the woman. Catherine's mothering of Cathy at the centre of the book relates past to present; projects present into future, so that past and future meet at source. The ethic of this feminine way of encountering reality is that of universal forgiveness; the metaphysic is one of final but mysterious redemption; the means of expression is that of a coded, secret utterance which, though we feel we understand fully while we read, has the knack akin to that of dream-language of slipping just out of comprehension when we awaken.

Toward the centre of *Wuthering Heights* occurs the transition where past meets future, youth meets age, death meets life. It is very like the structure of Shakespeare's tragi-comedies: "thou mettest with things dying, I with things new born," where, through the channel of labour from which a living girl-baby is drawn from the birth-canal of her dying mother we are led to brood upon the deepest mysteries of human existence: a living cycle which includes and transcends individual deaths and mortal-seeming bereavements. Emily Brontë starts chapter 2 of part 2 with a characteristic telling of the time: "About twelve o'clock, that night, was born the Catherine you saw at Wuthering Heights." She directs us to the moment of transition, the crucial turning point at which the threshold between two worlds is doubly crossed. The baby Catherine has come in; the mother Catherine's soul crosses with that of her child, on its way out. Twelve o'clock is the midpoint, at which the old day has given place to the new. All is grief and loss in this new day: the baby who has come in seems not, yet, to count. Nelly describes the aspect of Catherine lying dead as a scene of peace, but we do not always trust Nelly's evaluations, suspecting her of sentimentality at some times, as of vinegar sourness at others. Yet when she describes the moment of Catherine's departure to Heathcliff outside, there is a sense of perfect truthfulness:

> "How did she die?" . . .
> "Quietly as a lamb . . . she drew a sigh, and stretched herself, like a child reviving, and sinking again to sleep; and five minutes after I felt one little pulse at her heart, and nothing more."

Nelly is filling in information for Heathcliff, her head turned from Lockwood. She opens a window for us, into the immediate past, through which we have a chance of apprehending Catherine's last moments in this world. Emily Brontë constantly reveals just as tender and naturalistic an observation of the gestures and behaviour of babies and children as of the moorland creatures whose nature she knew by heart. If you have seen a little girl in a deep sleep, coming gently to the surface, perhaps roused by some dream, and then relapsing downward into the inner world without breaking the surface of consciousness, then you have seen Catherine's death as Emily Brontë meant you to imagine it. A child observed in sleep is poignant, existing in a remote world: to us who watch her, helpless, to herself unaware of being vulnerable, beyond the need for help. Nelly transmits an image of the soundest peace, in which the hearer may draw comfort as if from a well. In her telling, death has lost its sting; the grave its victory. She speaks of Catherine "sighing." A sigh which normally speaks to us of pain, is presented as the breath of life, prelude to "revival." We feel that Catherine does revive in some other world. The child goes home. Nelly touches Catherine's breast; records the final sign of life, "one little pulse." Her tenderness for this woman whom she has not much liked is shown quickened as Catherine, who has just borne a child, herself becomes one. As her daughter wakes into this world, we are given to believe that the mother wakens into another, as she had predicted and as Nelly feels constrained to echo: "Incomparably beyond and above you all." Nelly reinforces the idea of regression to childhood as the way out of the imprisoning mortal condition by going on to say that " 'her latest ideas wandered back to pleasant early days.' " The mighty circle of *Wuthering Heights,* in which the Hareton Earnshaw who built the Heights in 1500 returns to the Hareton Earnshaw who will marry this new young Cathy on January 1, 1803, is informed by smaller circles, leading us to muse on the final and original identity of "late" and "early"; first and last; mother and daughter. There is no linear path from present into the future, as if the world were laid out flat as a map; the map, Emily Brontë everywhere tells us, is a useful fiction which must not be mistaken for the shape of reality. In moving forward over the round world we recapitulate our mutual and personal history. Thus Nelly speaks of Catherine's "latest" thoughts (the last things) as "wandering back" to "early days" (her source and birth). To "wander" suggests those rambles on the moors which offered prospects of Paradise to Catherine and Heath-cliff, together with freedom from adult authority; to "wander" in mind means to go mad; to "wander back" means the joy of retracing steps without deliberate purpose but with the sure instinct of homing birds—like the pigeons Catherine has been seen feeding; of whose feathers in the stuffing of her pillows she had bitterly complained as keeping her soul hampered in the flesh. We are reminded too of Catherine's hallucination, when, going out of her mind at the onset of her illness, she had lost seven years of her life:

> I did not recall that they had been at all. I was a child; my father was just buried, and my misery arose from the separation that Hindley had ordered between me and Heathcliff—I was laid alone, for the first time.

In her delirium, Catherine had not managed to "wander back" far enough into childhood, but fell back only to the moment of exile which is a source of her present pain, confirmed by her own voluntary betrayal of Heathcliff for Linton at the age of seventeen. That return landed her in a sudden, inexplicable liaison with a "stranger; an exile, and outcast." Her wandering mind could do no more than settle her at the crucial moment of loss.

For Emily Brontë, the adult self is felt as a stray fragment of a greater whole, of which we may intensely dream or hallucinate, but not recover until we meet as children at our starting-point. For the elder Catherine, Heathcliff is this whole; for the younger, it will be Hareton to whom she goes home by some true instinct bred perhaps of the Linton tempering of her constitution, of her mother's mortal suffering, and of some maternal-seeming destiny suggested but never explained by the novel. In a last, deep relaxation of her fretful being, Catherine is shown by Nelly as being able to shed the years and be the child she was. In her poetry, Emily had many times implied this possibility. Near the eve of her coming-of-age, she speaks of the damp evening landscape "breathing of other years":

> Oh, I'm gone back to the days of youth,
> I am a child once more.

In an undated but probably late poem, she expressed the myth of going back which Catherine enacts in her dying moments, in a metaphor of going out on the moors which also includes the idea of wandering in mind:

> Often rebuked, yet always back returning
> To those first feelings that were born with me,
> And leaving busy chase of wealth and learning
> For idle dreams of things which cannot be:
>
> . . . .
>
> I'll walk where my own nature would be leading:
> It vexes me to choose another guide:
> Where the gray flocks in ferny glens are feeding;
> Where the wild wind blows on the mountain side.
>
> What have these lonely mountains worth revealing?
> More glory and more grief than I can tell:
> The earth which wakes *one* human heart to feeling
> Can centre both the worlds of Heaven and Hell.

Here the poet dramatizes the regressive process which she sees as the key to the sources of creativity and value by inverting the grammar: "turning back" becomes "back returning." "Often" is resisted by "always"; "rebuked" superseded by "return." In *Wuthering Heights,* Nelly enacts the adult world's "rebuke" of the child consciousness in man, which constantly performs an abrupt about-turn and goes sprinting back for home in accordance with the laws of its "own nature": " 'Give over with that baby-work! . . . Lie down and shut your eyes, you're wandering. There's a mess!' " Nelly spends most of her time expostulating as the lawless child-heroes give her the slip; wander off on the moors; push each other around; play serious games. To her infuriated demand that they grow up, they reply by silently eluding her grasp (as the second Cathy will do, by a stealth foreign to her guileless nature, to reach the Heights), and circling back to their starting-places. Heathcliff finally resists the onward pressure of time to move into the future by starving himself to death, until, "washed by rain," with his hand grazed upon the open window, and his unclosable dead eyes staring into the mortal world as his living eyes had gazed into the immortal one, he is placed with Catherine in the one grave. They sleep together. Over his grave, Hareton "with a streaming face" weeps like a child, not in proportion to the usage he received from the "sarcastic, savage" corpse he is burying, but according to the laws of his own strong and loving nature, and because he finds himself in some way kin to the foster-father who abuses him. Hareton is true to his childhood roots; Heathcliff returns to his, as the author holds we do return, not in a "second childhood" of senility, but first childhood, where we began.

Heathcliff himself, the destroyer, vengeful, avaricious, lying, and sadistic as he is, remains (especially at the moment of his most abject loss, in the centre of the book) profoundly and organically in touch with this process of recreation. He was the cuckoo in the nest who disturbed the world of the Heights, and outraged its symmetry of brother and sister balancing brother and sister at Thrushcross, whose intermarriage might in the course of things have taken place. He was the bane of Hindley and will be the potential undoing of Hareton. The only creation we can attribute to him is his sickly, spineless, and degenerate son, Linton Heathcliff, sired on Isabella in a fit of hate. Yet Heathcliff is associated by Emily Brontë with a kind of harmony and fertility which underlie all the other levels of order and disorder that superimpose in complex strata in the novel. Beneath the immaculate and fastidious social order symbolized by Thrushcross Grange and the Lintons' way of life, Catherine has discerned a predatory disorder, through her "baby-work" of undoing the pillow. At a yet deeper level, beneath the disharmony of Catherine's early death and Heathcliff's huge, inexplicable loss, is revealed a buried principle of a benign though pagan shaping-out of a destiny that is ultimately fruitful and kind. Emily Brontë allows us to glimpse this mysterious reparation which lies at the core of loss, through the most delicate allusions to the relationship between man and his natural setting, especially birds and trees. Nelly describes his appearance as she approaches him with the news of Catherine's death:

> He was there—at least a few yards further in the park; leant against an old ash tree, his hat off, and his hair soaked with the dew that had gathered on the budded branches, and fell pattering round him. He had been standing a long time in that position, for I saw a pair of ousels passing and repassing scarcely three feet from him, busy in building their nest, and regarding his proximity no more than that of a piece of timber. They flew off at my approach, and he raised his eyes and spoke:
> "She's dead!" he said.

It is spring. The buds in the ash in March are large and sticky; here they are covered in early-morning dew which overflows them on the bare head of the oblivious watcher beneath, keeping vigil. The ash is old, having seen many seasons. Heathcliff is felt to be deeply related to the surge of new life in the old stock, inevitably, subconsciously so. In Nelly's description, he seems to belong to the landscape as an intrinsic part of it—as if he were planted there, rooted not as a human and active entity but as a different species, quiet as the trees with which he is surrounded. He is recognized as a harmless part of nature by the inhabitants of the natural world going about their business—the ring ousels building their nest, who are not afraid to come within three feet of his stock-still body because they are ignorant that he is human and their natural enemy. They recognize Nelly sure enough, and depart. The ring ousels are emblems of fertility; in their pairing and nest-building they speak to us of the future. Emily Brontë will have known that this is a species in which both sexes build the nest, incubate and tend the brood; that they are related to the thrush (appropriate, then, to Thrushcross), and are reckless in protecting their young from predators. We remember the nest of little skeleton chicks over which Catherine mourned, and perhaps look forward to the later image of her daughter Cathy as a "bird flying back to a plundered nest which it had left brim-ful of chirping young ones." Heathcliff is a force causing such destruction to the young, yet here at the centre of the novel he seems to be imitating an opposite role. The ousels have returned early to their familiar nesting-site to build from the coarse grasses which they are conveying across Heath-cliff's line of vision. We are directed to the moment at the very turn of the year. Indoors the baby is new in its crib; the breeding birds are in a pair outside, building for the future. In this scene, the mateless Heathcliff—outside the human community, alongside these emblems of fidelity, the homing instinct, protectiveness, warmth—stands spiritless as "a piece of timber." Contrary to his own intentions, and against his will to destroy and uproot, he is in deep harmony with the scene, even a contributor to it.

In the second half of the novel, Heathcliff tries to thwart and mutilate the products of this fertility. Yet toward the end, it becomes clear that he cannot destroy anything; that he is in a strange way the agent of a harmony for which he cannot wish. Far from thieving the property of the Heights and the Grange from their rightful owners, his efforts marry the two in-heritances by bringing the two heirs into proximity. The "little dark thing, harboured by a good man to his bane" as Nelly muses, is not ultimately a "bane" at all, but an instrument of regeneration and of harmonious balance between eternal oppositions. *Wuthering Heights* hinges on a fruitful but—in rational terms—baffling paradox: order and disorder, creation and de-struction, being born and dying, looking in and seeing out, enclose and define each other, as if in a series of multiple parentheses. Within this pattern Heathcliff, for all his efficient manipulations, is caught static. He is, at the centre, a "piece of timber," rooted in the seasonal cycle, at whose foot the breeding birds are free to fulfil their instinctual nature. At the end of his career he is again static, ceasing to act because his cycle is fully lived out:

> I have to remind myself to breathe—almost to remind my heart to beat! And it is like bending back a stiff spring . . . it is by compulsion that I do the slightest act not prompted by one thought, and by compulsion that I notice anything alive or dead, which is not associated with one universal idea.

Under his very eyes, Hareton (" 'the ghost of my immortal love' ") and Cathy, who are in some respects so like himself and Catherine in their earlier lives, but tempered, reshaped and reshaping, are moving toward each other, to mate and build. Heathcliff is in process of turning back into the bedrock earth from whose rough nature he seems made: heath and cliff. Emily Brontë suggests a mode of existence intermediate between "human" and "nature," in which the subconscious continuum of our living—to breathe with our lungs, to pump the blood round with the heart—is coming to a deliberate standstill. Heathcliff, to stay alive at all, has to make a mental labour of the unthinking processes of survival. It is all said in the brilliant image of "bending back a stiff spring": incarnate existence has become to him a matter of mechanics predetermined to tend in an undesired direction. Nelly stresses in these latter moments of Heathcliff's life that he really does not seem quite human. But all she can suggest to explain him is that he might be a "goblin" or a "ghoul, or a vampire." She knows this to be very feeble and embarrassing when she reflects that she "had tended him in infancy," the vampire species having no known childhood. Joseph is much happier with his explanation when he shuffles in to view the corpse, announcing with malevolent joy that " 'Th' divil's harried off his soul.' " There is a beautifully wry note in Nelly's description of Joseph as "the old sinner," as he grins back at his master's face set in rigor mortis, and, labelling him a fiend, looks ready to dance for joy all round the deathbed. When Heathcliff is buried, Nelly feels anxious that he bears no surname, simply the one (surely not a "Christian") name, which is inscribed simply and singly upon his gravestone. Heathcliff has moved from a death-in-life to a life-in-death with Catherine. He has passed through the window; reverted, as Gimmerton Kirk will do, to the moor. Personality is annulled, but a new, impersonal, more absolutely vital existence is felt to begin as the heath which is his original claims its namesake.

At the centre, Nelly, having seen Catherine on her passage out of the world and Cathy on her way in, enters the park expecting that Heathcliff had been out "among the larches" all night. It is characteristic of the author to name the species of tree rather than to refer to generalized trees. The larch is a fir but not ever-green, shedding needles annually from delicate, slender boughs and with the spring reclothing itself in soft pale-green. Midway between the evergreen and deciduous worlds, it looks like the one, behaves like the other. Heathcliff is absorbed in his waiting into the wood. He beats his head against the trunk of the ash in his agony: "I observed several splashes of blood about the bark of the tree, and his hand and forehead were both stained; probably the scene I witnessed was a repetition of others enacted during the night." This extreme behaviour has often been seen as a bizarre intrusion of Gothic in which the obligatory maniac behaves like a howling beast rather than a man. But there is a deeper, mythic meaning to these actions. Heathcliff now has a double nature: he both lives and does not live. Catherine, who is conceived of as his own being will be buried and he left above ground, "with his soul in the grave." In this absolute loss he meets the boundaries of human nature but cannot get across. Nelly sees him as an animal. It is easier for her to formulate the idea of the nonhuman in these terms. The breeding birds see him as a tree. We see his blood shed upon the bark of the ash and staining it; his forehead too is stained with blood as if baptismally. In the image of the blood-stained tree Emily Brontë suggests an analogy to the sacrificial slaughter either of animal or man, by which the ancient mystery religions sought to appease the deities and ensure a fruitful new year. Heathcliff's pain is absolutely acute. The year, the hour, the day turn; the baby is born, the birds mate. The old mother passes, while the man's blood, like that of the sacrifical king of ancient pagan religions, seeps into mother earth.

The happiness of the future, Emily Brontë asserts, is built on the destruction of the past, and is seen by the reader to depend on it. In one of the most poignantly beautiful images of *Wuthering Heights,* stated matter-of-factly two chapters later, Nelly says of the second Catherine, whose birth had killed her mother: "For the rest, after the first six months, she grew like a larch; and could walk and talk too, in her own way, before the heath blossomed a second time over Mrs. Linton's dust." "Six months" takes us to September, the year's turning into winter: Cathy has it in her to resist and overcome winter. Since the moorland heather blooms in August to September, the same sentence takes us through yet another full cycle, placing an image of hope and renewal (the purple bells of heather) directly upon an image of loss and mortality (Mrs. Linton reduced to "dust"). The child has in her the best of the Lintons and the best of the Earnshaws, in fruitful mixture. If she is "like" her mother she is also "like" Heathcliff, since we must believe Catherine's conviction that "I *am* Heathcliff." As he stood in the terrible night of Cathy's birth amongst the larches, and shed his blood upon the bark of a tree, so Cathy "grew like a larch." In some mysterious way, Heathcliff is intrinsically linked to the second Cathy, and has given up some of his life to her.

Chronology

1812   The Reverend Patrick Brontë marries Maria Branwell.

1814   Maria Brontë, their first child, born.

1815   Elizabeth Brontë born.

1816   Charlotte Brontë born on April 21.

1817   Patrick Branwell Brontë, the only son, born in June.

1818   Emily Jane Brontë born, July 30.

1820   Anne Brontë born, January 17. The Brontë family moves to the parsonage at Haworth, near Bradford, Yorkshire.

1821   Mrs. Brontë dies of cancer in September. Her sister, Elizabeth Branwell, takes charge of the household.

1824   Maria and Elizabeth attend the Clergy Daughters' School at Cowan Bridge. Charlotte follows them in August, and Emily in November.

1825   The two oldest girls, Maria and Elizabeth, contract tuberculosis at school. Maria dies on May 6; Elizabeth dies June 15. Charlotte and Emily are withdrawn from the school on June 1. Charlotte and Emily do not return to school until they are in their teens; in the meantime they are educated at home.

1826   Rev. Brontë brings home a box of wooden soldiers for his son; this is the catalyst for the creation of the Brontës' juvenile fantasy worlds and writings. Charlotte and Branwell begin the "Angrian" stories and magazines; Emily and Anne work on the "Gondal" saga.

1831   Charlotte attends Miss Wooler's school. She leaves the school seven months later, to tend to her sisters' education. In 1835, however, she returns as governess. She is accompanied by Emily.

1835   After only three months, Emily leaves Miss Wooler's school because of homesickness. Anne arrives in January 1836, and remains until December 1837.

1837   In September, Emily becomes governess at Miss Patchett's school, near Halifax.

1838   In May, Charlotte leaves her position at Miss Wooler's school.

1839   Anne becomes governess for the Ingram family at Blake Hall, Mirfield. She leaves in December. Charlotte becomes governess in the Sidwick family, at Stonegappe Hall, near Skipton. She leaves after two months (July).

1840   All three sisters live at Haworth.

1841   Anne becomes governess in the Robinson family, near York. Charlotte becomes governess in the White family and moves to Upperwood House, Rawdon. She leaves in December. The sisters plan to start their own school. The scheme, attempted several years later, fails for lack of inquiries.

1842   Charlotte and Emily travel to Brussels to study in the Pensionnat Héger. Here, Charlotte suffers unrequited love for the master of the school, M. Héger. Upon the death of their aunt in November, they return to Haworth.

1843   Branwell joins Anne in York as tutor to the Robinson family. Charlotte returns to Brussels and remains until January 1844.

1845   Charlotte discovers Emily's poetry and suggests that a selection be published along with the poetry of herself and Anne.

1846   *Poems, by Currer, Ellis, and Acton Bell* published by Aylott & Jones. Two copies are sold. Charlotte's *The Professor,* Emily's *Wuthering Heights,* and Anne's *Agnes Grey* are all completed. The latter two are accepted by T. C. Newby, but *The Professor* is rejected. Charlotte's *Jane Eyre* is begun in August and immediately accepted by Smith, Elder & Co. upon its completion in August of 1847.

1847   *Jane Eyre* published. *Wuthering Heights* and *Agnes Grey* published by T. C. Newby.

1848   Anne's *The Tenant of Wildfell Hall* published by T. C. Newby, who tries to sell it to an American publisher as a new book by Currer Bell, author of the immensely popular *Jane Eyre.* Smith, Elder & Co. requests that Charlotte bring her sisters to London to prove that there are three Bells. Charlotte and Anne visit London. Branwell dies of tuberculosis, September 24. Emily dies of the same, December 19.

1849   Anne dies of tuberculosis, May 28.

1850   Charlotte edits her sisters' work. Smith, Elder & Co. publishes a new edition of *Wuthering Heights* and *Agnes Grey,* along with some of Anne's and Emily's poetry, and a "Biographical Notice" of her sisters' lives by Charlotte.

Contributors

HAROLD BLOOM, Sterling Professor of the Humanities at Yale University, is the author of *The Anxiety of Influence, Poetry and Repression,* and many other volumes of literary criticism. His forthcoming study, *Freud: Transference and Authority,* attempts a full-scale reading of all of Freud's major writings. A MacArthur Prize Fellow, he is general editor of five series of literary criticism published by Chelsea House.

DOROTHY VAN GHENT taught at Kansas University and the University of Vermont. Her numerous publications include *The English Novel: Form and Function* and *Keats: The Myth of the Hero.*

DAVID SONSTROEM is Professor of English at the University of Connecticut at Storrs.

FRANK KERMODE is Professor of English at Columbia University. He is the author of *D. H. Lawrence, The Sense of an Ending,* and *Forms of Attention.*

MARGARET HOMANS is Associate Professor of English at Yale University. Her publications include *Women Writers and Poetic Identity: Dorothy Wordsworth, Emily Brontë, and Emily Dickinson.*

SANDRA M. GILBERT is Professor of English at Princeton University. Together with Susan Gubar, she has written *The Madwoman in the Attic* and edited *The Norton Anthology of Women's Literature* and *Shakespeare's Sisters: Feminist Essays on Women Poets.*

CAROL JACOBS is Professor of English and Comparative Literature at the State University of New York at Buffalo and the author of *The Dissimulating Harmony.*

STEVIE DAVIES is the author of *Images of Kinship in* Paradise Lost, *Renaissance Views of Man,* and *Emily Brontë: The Artist as Free Woman;* and the editor of *The Brontë Sisters: Selected Poems.*

139

Bibliography

Allott, Miriam, ed. *The Brontë's: The Critical Heritage*. London and Boston: Routledge & Kegan Paul, 1974.

————. Wuthering Heights: *A Casebook*. London: Macmillan, 1970.

Anderson, Walter E. "The Lyrical Form of *Wuthering Heights*." *Toronto University Quarterly* 47 (1977–78): 112–34.

Bataille, Georges. *Literature and Evil*. Translated by Alastair Hamilton. New York: Marion Boyars, 1985.

Benvenuto, Richard. *Emily Brontë*. Boston: Twayne, 1982.

Bersani, Leo. *A Future for Astyanax: Character and Desire in Literature*. London: Marion Boyars, 1978.

Blondel, Jacques. *Emily Brontë: Experience Spirituelle et Creation Poetique*. Paris: Presses Universitaires de France, 1955.

Bloom, Harold, ed. *Modern Critical Views: The Brontës*. New Haven: Chelsea House, 1986.

Brick, Allen R. "*Wuthering Heights:* Narrators, Audience and Message." *College English* 21 (November 1959): 80–86.

Buckley, Vincent, "Passion and Control in *Wuthering Heights*." *The Southern Review* 1 (1964): 5–23.

Cecil, David. *Victorian Novelists: Essays in Revaluation*. London: Constable, 1948.

Chase, Richard. "The Brontës, or, Myth Domesticated." In *Forms of Modern Fiction: Essays Collected in Honor of Joseph Warren Beach,* edited by William Van O'Connor. Bloomington: Indiana University Press, 1962.

Craik, W. A. *The Brontë Novels*. London: Methuen, 1968.

Daiches, David. "Introduction." In *Wuthering Heights*. London: Penguin, 1965.

Davies, Stevie. *Emily Brontë: The Artist as a Free Woman*. Manchester, England: Carcanet Press, 1983.

De Grazia, Emilio. "The Ethical Dimension of *Wuthering Heights*." *Midwest Quarterly* 19 (Winter 1978): 178–95.

Dingle, Herbert. *The Mind of Emily Brontë*. London: Martin Brian & O'Keeffe, 1974.

Donoghue, Denis. "Emily Brontë: On the Latitude of Interpretation." In *The Interpretation of Narrative: Theory and Practice,* edited by Morton W. Bloomfield. Cambridge: Harvard University Press, 1970.

Dry, Florence Swinton. *The Sources of* Wuthering Heights. Cambridge, England: W. Heffer & Sons, 1937.

Eagleton, Terry. *Myths of Power: A Marxist Study of the Brontës*. London: Macmillan, 1975.

Ewbank, Inga-Stina. *Their Proper Sphere: A Study of the Brontë Sisters as Early-Victorian Female Novelists*. London: Edward Arnold, 1966.

Goetz, William R. "Genealogy and Incest in *Wuthering Heights*." *Studies in the Novel* 14, no. 4 (Winter 1982): 359–76.

Gose, Elliott B., Jr. *Imagination Indulged: The Irrational in the Nineteenth-Century Novel*. Montreal: McGill, Queen's University Press, 1972.

Gregor, Ian, ed. *The Brontës: A Collection of Critical Essays*. Englewood Cliffs, N.J.: Prentice-Hall, 1970.

Hardwick, Elizabeth. *Seduction and Betrayal: Women and Literature*. New York: Random House, 1974.

Hewish, John. *Emily Brontë: A Critical and Biographical Study*. London: Macmillan, 1969.

Hinkley, Laura L. *The Brontës: Charlotte and Emily*. New York: Hastings House, 1946.

Homans, Margaret. "Dreaming of Children: Literalization in *Jane Eyre* and *Wuthering Heights*." In *The Female Gothic,* edited by Judith E. Fleenor, 257–79. Montreal: Eden, 1983.

Kettle, Arnold. *An Introduction to the English Novel*. Vol. 1. London: Hutchinson University Library, 1951.

Kiely, Robert. *The Romantic Novel in England*. Cambridge: Harvard University Press, 1972.

Knoepflmacher, U. C. *Laughter and Despair: Reading in Ten Novels of the Victorian Era*. Berkeley and Los Angeles: University of California Press, 1971.

Krupat, Arnold. "The Strangeness of *Wuthering Heights*." *Nineteenth-Century Fiction* 25 (December 1970): 269–80.

Leavis, Q. D. "A Fresh Approach to *Wuthering Heights*." In *Lectures in America,* by F. R. Leavis and Q. D. Leavis. New York: Pantheon, 1969.

Matthews, John T. "Framing in *Wuthering Heights,*" *Texas Studies in Literature and Language* 27, no. 1 (Spring 1985): 25–61.

Mathison, John K. "Nelly Dean and the Power of *Wuthering Heights*." *Nineteenth-Century Fiction* 11 (September 1956): 106–29.

McCarthy, Terence. "The Incompetent Narrator of *Wuthering Heights*." *Modern Language Quarterly* 42, no. 1 (March 1981): 48–64.

McKibben, Robert C. "The Image of the Book in *Wuthering Heights*." *Nineteenth-Century Fiction* 15 (September 1960): 159–69.

Miller, J. Hillis. *The Disappearance of God: Five Nineteenth-Century Writers*. New York: Schocken, 1965.

———. *The Form of Victorian Fiction*. Notre Dame, Ind.: University of Notre Dame Press, 1968.

Moser, Thomas. "What Is the Matter with Emily Jane? Conflicting Impulses in *Wuthering Heights*." *Nineteenth-Century Fiction* 17 (June 1962): 1–19.

Oates, Joyce Carol. "The Magnanimity of *Wuthering Heights*." *Critical Inquiry* 9, no. 2 (December 1982): 435–49.

Ohmann, Carol. "Emily Brontë in the Hands of Male Critics." *College English* 32 (May 1971): 906–13.

Pinion, F. B. *A Brontë Companion: Literary Assessment, Background, and Reference.* London: Macmillan, 1975.

Ratchford, Fannie Elizabeth. *The Brontës' Web of Childhood.* New York: Columbia University Press, 1941.

Sale, William M., Jr., ed. *Emily Brontë:* Wuthering Heights. A Norton Critical Edition. New York: Norton, 1963.

Schorer, Mark. "Fiction and the 'Matrix of Analogy.' " *The Kenyon Review* 11, no. 4 (Autumn 1949): 539–60.

Sinclair, May. *The Three Brontës.* Boston and New York: Houghton Mifflin, 1912.

Smith, Anne. *The Art of Emily Brontë.* London: Vision Press, 1976.

Spark, Muriel, and Derek Stanford. *Emily Brontë: Her Life and Work.* New York: Coward-McCann, 1966.

Stevenson, W. H. "*Wuthering Heights:* The Facts." *Essays in Criticism* 14, no. 2 (April 1985): 149–66.

Stone, Donald D. *The Romantic Impulse in Victorian Fiction.* Cambridge: Harvard University Press, 1980.

Tanner, Tony. "Passion, Narrative and Identity in *Wuthering Heights* and *Jane Eyre.*" In *Teaching the Text,* edited by Susanne Kappeler and Norman Bryson. London: Routledge & Kegan Paul, 1983.

Tillotson, Kathleen. *Novels of the 1840s.* Oxford: Clarendon, 1954.

Visick, Mary. *The Genesis of* Wuthering Heights. Hong Kong: Hong Kong University Press, 1958.

Winnifrith, Tom. *The Brontës and Their Background: Romance and Reality.* London: Macmillan, 1973.

Woolf, Virginia. *The Common Reader,* 1st ser. London: Hogarth Press, 1925.

Acknowledgments

"On *Wuthering Heights*" by Dorothy Van Ghent from *The English Novel: Form and Function* by Dorothy Van Ghent, © 1953 by Dorothy Van Ghent. Reprinted by permission of Holt, Rinehart & Winston.

"*Wuthering Heights* and the Limits of Vision" by David Sonstroem from *PMLA* 86, no. 1 (January 1971), © 1971 by the Modern Language Association of America. Reprinted by permission.

"A Modern Way with the Classic" (originally entitled "IV: atque hic ingentem comitatum/ adfluxisse novorum/ invenio admirans numerum. . .") by Frank Kermode from *The Classic: Literary Images of Permanence and Change* by Frank Kermode, © 1975, 1983 by Frank Kermode. Reprinted by permission of the author and Literistic, Ltd. This essay originally appeared as "A Modern Way with the Classic" in New Literary History 5, no. 3 (Spring 1974) © 1973 by New Literary History. Reprinted by permission of the Johns Hopkins University Press.

"Repression and Sublimation of Nature in *Wuthering Heights*" by Margaret Homans from *PMLA* 93, no. 1 (January 1978), © 1978 by the Modern Language Association of America. Reprinted by permission.

"Looking Oppositely: Catherine Earnshaw's Fall" by Sandra M. Gilbert from *The Madwoman in the Attic: The Woman Writer and the Nineteenth Century Literary Imagination* by Sandra M. Gilbert and Susan Gubar, © 1979 by Yale University. Reprinted by permission of the author and Yale University Press.

"*Wuthering Heights:* At the Threshold of Interpretation" by Carol Jacobs from *boundary 2* 7, no. 3 (Spring 1979), © 1979 by *boundary 2*. Reprinted by permission of *boundary 2: a journal of postmodern literature and culture*.

"Baby-Work: The Myth of Rebirth in *Wuthering Heights*" by Stevie Davies from *Emily Bronte: The Artist as a Free Woman* by Stevie Davies, © 1983 by Stevie Davies. Reprinted by permission of Carcanet Press Ltd.

145

Index